Awakened Mind

One-Minute Wake Up Calls
to a Bold and Mindful Life

David Kundtz

Conari Press

First published in 2009 by Conari Press,
an imprint of Red Wheel/Weiser, LLC
With offices at:
500 Third Street, Suite 230
San Francisco, CA 94107
www.redwheelweiser.com

ISBN: 978-1-57324-360-5

Library of Congress Cataloging-in-Publication Data
Kundtz, David.
Awakened mind: one-minute wake up calls to a bold and mindful life/
David Kundtz.
    p. cm.
 1. Generosity. 2. Awareness. I. Title.
  BJ1533.G4K86 2009
  158—dc22
                    2008046111

Cover and interior design by Maija Tollefson
Cover photograph © Vladimir Grekov
Author photograph © John Lomibao

Printed in Canada
TCP
10 9 8 7 6 5 4 3 2 1

In Gratitude
To so many for so much

Beyond living and dreaming
there is something more important:
waking up.

—Antonio Machado

Table of Contents

Preface: Terrible Innocence

You can't wake a person who is pretending to be asleep.

—American Navajo Proverb

When I was a psychology student, I was fortunate to take a class from Daniel Berrigan, the renowned Jesuit peace activist, teacher, and author. What I remember most from that short course so many years ago is a term he used: terrible innocence.

Terrible innocence is an attitude that allows us, while looking into the face of evil and harmful things, to deny or avoid their existence, pretend not to notice them, feign ignorance about their true nature, or pretend they have nothing to do with us. It is fooling ourselves because the reality is too inconvenient, too alien, or too scary to deal with directly and honestly. It is, as the Navajo say, pretending to be asleep.

The trait that distinguishes terrible innocence from simple innocence is consciousness. The truly innocent are indeed naïve about the realities they face; in this sense, they are really asleep. In the case of children, they have not yet awakened. Terribly innocent adults know, however, in some deep chamber of the heart, in some dark corner of the soul, what's what. They are not truly asleep. They are pretending; that's what makes it terrible. This brings the false innocence of sweetness and light to a moment we know, on some level of consciousness, is potentially very bad business. It is make-believe.

We do it all the time. It's a very human thing to do.

It is so tempting, for example, to exclude yourself from concern about, even from interest in, certain negative topics or certain groups of people simply because you don't see yourself as part of them. If you don't belong to a racial minority, or a sexual minority—if you are not poor or living in exile, or illiterate, or uneducated, or physically handicapped, or chronically ill, or oppressed, or tortured, or . . . on and on—you may, with no conscious ill-will, be thinking something like: "This particular issue really has nothing to do with me."

That's it! That's a perfect example terrible innocence.

Only when we *all* identify with *all* of us, will we *all* get along and thrive. The racism that does not seem to affect you, the anti-gay sentiment that simply has nothing to do with you, are in fact of urgent importance to you. Because what happens to any of us happens to all of us.

When you really get that idea, your life changes.

Thus the purpose of these reflections is to encourage you to cultivate and deepen an awakened mind that is willing to delve into the deep chambers and dark corners—and some not so deep and not so dark—to challenge the terrible innocence we may bring to what is inconvenient, or scary, or seemingly irrelevant or alien to our lives. These reflections can help you transform that terrible innocence into an effective and spirited meeting of whatever needs to be met, of dealing with whatever you are trying to avoid.

The converse of terrible innocence is courageous embrace. To embrace what is difficult is also a very human thing to do; indeed, it is a more nobly human thing to do. As the Navajo proverb says, when you pretend you are asleep, no one can awaken you. You must stop the pretending and awaken yourself, transforming your terrible innocence into a "bold and mindful life," a life aware of and responsive to what's really going on, to what's often hiding "between the lines" and "below the surface," and to what ultimately nourishes your values and gives you meaning.

David Kundtz
Vancouver, British Columbia

CHAPTER 1

Thanks and Generosity

—:: —

Forgiven?

It is easier to forgive an enemy than a friend.

—Dorothée Deluzy

He was a friend. We worked together and had known each other for several years. We occasionally met at social and other functions and regularly spent time in conversation.

One day, he asked to borrow 500 dollars from me. He needed it very badly for something very important, implying it was for one of his children. He was, at the moment only, without enough liquid assets; he would pay me back very soon. I was taken off guard because it was the last thing I expected to hear from him. I loaned him the money. Never saw it again. Although I did see him, as regularly as ever—which was a problem.

He often promised to pay the loan back—soon, in just a day or so, or at the beginning of the next week, or whatever. Eventually, he stopped saying anything about it and just avoided me as much as he could. Very awkward.

Then I found out. He gambled. The horses. Oh.

From the day of the loan to this, it has been difficult for me to forgive him. I have wondered why. When I read the saying above, I found an answer. He was a friend! Yet he stole from me and he lied to me!

In retrospect, I realize that I was basically asleep in this situation. Had I been more awake to the reality around me, I would have known, as many others did, not to lend this guy money because he'd simply gamble it away. Lesson one.

Lesson two is about the forgiving thing. If someone I didn't know had stolen the money from me, I could have let it go more easily and theoretically "forgiven" some anonymous person out there with my money. But this was a friend. It touches on trust, security, self-worth, self-image, the way we relate to others, and a whole lot more. I'm still trying to wake up about this one.

> *Like me, is there a friend you need or want to forgive?*

Wounded Soldier

— :: —

Without your wounds where would your power be? The very angels themselves cannot persuade the wretched and blundering children on earth as can one human being broken in the wheels of living. In love's service, only the wounded soldiers can serve.

— Thornton Wilder

There was a time around mid-life when I was, to put it mildly, at sixes and sevens. I was seriously questioning the major systems of my life: spiritual, relational, and material. The most painful and most fearful part was that I really had no idea how it would all turn out—that is, how *I* would turn out. Would I get through this? And would I be able to keep close to my values, my friends, and my family? I honestly did not know the answers to these doubts.

To whom can I go? I asked myself. From whom will I receive the wisdom and understanding that I so desperately need right now? There were many well-suited advisors nearby. My answer, however, was intuitive and clear: a friend and mentor of my youth, now an old man and on the other coast, a "wounded soldier" who had been through many battles in several wars, which had bestowed on him an immense moral power. "An old war horse" is what he called himself.

What I received from him was not any identifiable piece of advice, but rather a lot of listening, a lot of smiling, a lot of tea-offering, a lot of understanding, and a lot of affirming. "You'll get through this just fine," he said. Yet I don't recall that he actually used those words.

My most vivid memory of a more-than-two-hour conversation in a quiet booth in an empty restaurant in Washington, D.C. is of hunting for his car afterward. We both totally lost track of where he had parked and we spent fully a half hour laughing and walking up and down the streets of Georgetown in search of it. Absent-minded? A bit, yes, in regard to parking. But a 100 percent present to me.

> *Who is a wounded soldier in your life? Or maybe:*
> *For whom are you a wounded soldier?*

Gratitude

—::—

Gratitude unlocks the fullness of life. It turns what we have into enough, and more. It turns denial into acceptance, chaos to order, confusion to clarity. It can turn a meal into a feast, a house into a home, a stranger into a friend. Gratitude makes sense of our past, brings peace for today, and creates a vision for tomorrow.

—Melody Beattie

Wow, that's really giving gratitude a lot of power. And, I believe, rightly so.

To understand the power gratitude has to bestow contentment, you need only accept that it has nothing to do with the length of your list of things for which you are grateful. The length of your theoretical list—or even if you've actually made one—is quite subjective. Rather it is your attitude toward the whole of life, no matter what it brings, that signifies.

I have known people who are over-abundantly blessed with the world's goods and powers and yet do not live in gratitude. I have also known those who live with a great poverty of goods and powers who do. What a difference a "thanks" makes.

She was a very old woman who knew she was soon to die. She lived her entire life in abject poverty. Her husband and two of her four children were already dead. She always had a smile and a good word. She entrusted to me her gold wedding band, worn thin over the years, the only thing of value she owned. She asked me to sell it and do something good with the proceeds. "I have been very blessed by God," she said, "and my heart is full of gratitude." She died within a month.

Her list of "Things I Am Thankful For" was long, practically endless; although, if I had been asked to make that list for her, it would have been short indeed. The point, of course, is that it was *her* list, it was *her* life, and it was *her* choice of what attitude to bring to it.

> *Soon, turn what you have into enough: a stranger into a friend, a meal into a feast. We all thank you.*

Suffer With

—::—

The whole idea of compassion is based on a keen aware-
ness of the interdependence of all . . . living beings,
which are all part of one another, and all involved in
one another.

—Thomas Merton

Compassion: sympathetic consciousness of others' dis-
tress together with a desire to alleviate it; from the Latin
through the French and Middle English: *com* (with) *pati*
(to bear, suffer). Thus, to suffer with. What a beautiful
word!

She was someone I knew casually. I would have
had to consider carefully, had I been asked at the time,
if she were a friend or an acquaintance. Soon, however,
I knew she was a friend. That's because of her compassion. I'll call her Angela.

I had just suffered a rather serious loss, the death
of a close friend who lived in a distant city. I was not
able, for various reasons, to go and be there. None of
the people in my current life knew this friend and thus
were not personally affected by his death.

Somehow Angela knew the pain I was carrying and the depth of the loss I was feeling. I say "somehow," but it was clear why she understood: she had been there herself. But so had many people I knew; many had suffered the loss of a friend. What Angela had was compassion, the combination of understanding what I was carrying because of a similar experience and a lack of fear to approach and share my deep emotion. It's the latter ingredient in compassion that is challenging for most of us. How I appreciated her willingness *not* to stay away from my pain, *not* to "give me space" to grieve when what I needed was someone to share my pain and my grief.

As Merton says, compassion is based on a keen awareness—an awareness that is willing to act—that we are "all involved in one another." Angela's compassion brought her to look me in the eye, to stay with me and not leave, and to be an understanding listener. What a gift.

> *Find someone to "suffer with." You probably won't have to look far.*

Integrity

—::—

Don't pray when it rains if you don't pray when the sun shines.

—Satchel Paige

Satchel is really talking about more than prayer. Giving his comment a positive spin, he's talking about integrity; giving it a negative one, he's talking about hypocrisy.

The comical, lovable, and talented baseball player (Cleveland Indians, c.1948) was just "sayin' it like he saw it." You can't have it both ways if you want to be true to yourself.

When I was boy, I was strongly encouraged to pray for a particular day to be sunny. It was presented to me as both important and necessary; so, of course, I did it.

The day in question was that of the springtime garden party to benefit the Carmelite nuns. It was to be held on the grounds of their monastery. Both my mother and aunt were active presenters of this event and its success meant a great deal to the cloistered nuns who benefited from it. (They, of course, did not attend, being cloistered. Seemed very unfair to me. I often wondered if they looked through the windows to see how the party was going.)

At other times, I also prayed for snow—so much snow that school would be cancelled.

These prayers seem naïve now. They have a feeling of times gone by and simpler assumptions about a lot of things. However, at the time, they seemed both real and honest—and, for many, they may still be.

I don't pray about the weather any more, but I still like Satchel's advice. If you pray for the rain to stop, you gotta say thanks for the sun or *vice versa*. It's one of the marks of an integrated life. It encourages you to get out of yourself and think in broader terms about living your human life in the community of others.

Here's another way of thinking about Satchel's advice: A "please" is best followed by a "thank you."

... and a "thank you" by a "you're welcome."

Innocence

— :: —

Children always understand. They have open minds.
They have built-in shit detectors.

—Madonna

Bigger-than-life Madonna captures, in her own outspoken way, a trait of childhood that we all recognize: innocence and a lack of worldly experience that betrays little or no sarcasm, irony, disdain, or cynicism. Very appealing in most cases; sometimes revealing. After an embarrassing or awkward moment, adults circumlocute and prevaricate and euphemize. Children simply tell the accurate and unvarnished truth, like the following comment (told to me by a friend): "Grandma, you have hair in your nose."

What happens to children to make them become prevaricators and euphemizers rather than truth-tellers? It's inevitable, isn't it? Maybe necessary? However, I would like to hold out for keeping at least a vestige of childhood's truth-telling and "innocence."

I use quotes around that word, because it is not true innocence in most adults; it's more like what French philosopher Paul Ricoeur called the second naïveté. This is not "terrible innocence," but rather an attitude that, while knowing and having experienced the reality of the world (therefore, not truly or blindly naïve), we choose to perceive reality with the eyes of someone more innocent. It operates out of consciousness and implies trust and good will—which can also get you into trouble, as you have to have wisdom as well.

I recall times when I did not have the necessary wisdom (my vulnerability leans more toward the naïve rather than the cynical) and I paid the price. I was left holding the bag or its equivalent.

Isn't balance the adult goal here? On the one hand, a trust and basic assumption of goodwill that is the vestige of childhood innocence; on the other, a wariness and sophistication sufficient to spot and foil the bad-willed.

I've just come from an enjoyable holiday weekend with family and friends. Among them was a seven-year-old boy. What a joy he was to talk with, observe, and generally marvel at! Innocence! Open mind! And equipped with Madonna's "detector," too.

Find a kid. Observe! Awaken to a new "innocence."

Friend

—::—

When we honestly ask ourselves which person . . . means the most to us, we often find it is those who, instead of giving much advice . . . have chosen rather to share our pain and touch our wounds with a gentle and tender hand.

—Henri Nouwen

Most people, it seems to me, have the feeling that they are much more frequently a friend to others than they are the recipient of others' friendship. How do you feel about that?

If this is true for you, I have a hunch why. Our expression of friendship is often too soft, too weakly expressed, too timid and thus easily not noticed, misread, or otherwise overlooked. We seem to live in a culture that doesn't want to butt in or invade anyone's privacy, sometimes to an extreme.

I think this is an area where we need to eschew caution and timidity and barge right in with friendship.

I was at a convention gathering—the newbie in the group who didn't know anyone—and I felt isolated.

Everyone seemed to know everyone else, all standing around in groups chatting and laughing animatedly like friends; everyone but me.

I searched for another single individual I could approach for conversation and thus join the group. I saw no one. I was becoming self-conscious when I felt a touch on my shoulder ("a gentle and tender hand") from behind. I turned to encounter an elderly woman with a kind face smiling and saying, "We've just been saying that there seem to be so many people here from the West this year. Where are you from?" as she drew me into her conversational group.

That was it. My feelings of isolation were transformed into feelings of inclusion. I felt part of the group immediately.

It was a small thing, an easy gesture on her part. In that moment, she was a friend to me. A small thing, yes, but I still remember it.

> *Be awake to opportunities to reach out a "gentle and tender hand."*

Honesty with Humor

—— :: ——

I've had a perfectly wonderful evening. But this wasn't it.

—Groucho Marx

I seem to find myself in many situations in which I question whether or not to say what I am actually thinking, or for some reason—always perceived to be justified—to avoid, to dither, to dissemble, even to lie.

Do I tell well-loved relatives what I think of their political opinions or keep my thoughts to myself?

Do I express my feelings about a particular manifestation of religious fervor or just let it go?

When a friend proudly shows me a newly bought painting, do I say what I think, that it's abominable? Say nothing? Change the topic? When my hostess asks if I liked her squid bouillabaisse, what do I say?

Most of the time, when I try to straddle the line between a negative truth and a cover-up, my decision proves unsatisfactory. I either offend or prevaricate.

Enter Groucho—with humor (not that I recommend his comment above to any host). Is there a way

I can actually tell the truth, softening it with humor, kindness, understanding? Thus:

"It's a good thing we love one another or our political differences would do us in!"

"You know there are some experiences in the religious history of each of us at which we can all laugh or that we all have in common."

"It's wonderful! You've found a work of art that speaks deeply to you and graces your home!"

"My dear, the bouillabaisse was exceptional, but the charm of the hostess outshines every aspect of the evening."

No, I can't hear myself saying those things, either. But let's keep trying.

Care

— :: —

How you do anything is how you do everything.

—Zen Master

I had just finished my training as a psychotherapist and was enthusiastic about beginning a career as a family counselor. A key element in my training were my clinical supervisors—one especially whom I admired and valued.

The thought came to me that this person, who was a skilled, insightful, and charismatic therapist, could be doing any kind of work and would still be skilled, insightful, and charismatic. Because that's who he was, in himself. You could change his training and his work, and he would be the same; whether a business man, a lawyer, a farmer, a social worker, a fireman, or a therapist, he would be skilled, insightful, and charismatic.

Granted, certain kinds of work fit certain kinds of personalities, but, for the most part, *how you do anything is how you do everything.*

I believe the thought holds true, for the most part, within the lives of us all. How you wash the dishes tells me something about the kind of physician you may be. How you make the bed is how you will practice law. How my accountant keeps his home says something about how he will keep his books. How a woman presents herself to the world tells me something about the quality of her nursing. The way a carpenter treats his tools says much about his work.

Always pay attention to the feel of the office space when you look for a therapist. It has nothing to do with amount of money spent, with sophisticated or common tastes; it has to do with the quality of care.

And the same, of course, is true for me—and you. Do we care? Whether we are making life-altering interventions or performing day-to-day tasks to maintain family life, do we care?

> *Sublime endeavor or dreaded drudgery. How you do anything . . . .*

Aging

— :: —

Threescore and ten I can remember well:
Within the volume of which time I have seen
Hours dreadful and things strange. . .

—William Shakespeare

I take the Bard's words for my own—and add few thoughts as my threescore and ten moves inexorably on.

Yes, I have seen dreadful and strange things, but probably no more than others my age. The fact is that we have all seen too many dreadful things.

Yet, as I grow older, I continue to believe—at some moments more than others—that, in the long view, the world is getting better in many ways. I know there are significant arguments against this, not the least of which point to the frequency and proliferation of violence and poverty throughout the world.

One attitude that has not improved—has, in fact, worsened, if you ask me—is our attitude toward getting old. The term itself, "getting old," has a very negative sound to our ears. Old age is wrapped in euphemisms. Most people don't even use the word "old" when talking about others, substituting "elderly," or "senior citizens." "You're only as old as you feel," they say. No, you're as old as you are; you feel as old as you feel.

The young don't—can't?—see themselves when they look at old people, which I suppose is simply human nature.

In our youth-focused culture, it has become negative to be old. Think about that for a moment. How did we get so wrong-headed? Stupid, really, since old age is the lot of the fortunate who survive to enjoy it. More important, it is the time when you've been around long enough to know a few things. Despite all the losses it can imply, and there are plenty, I can number several unique joys of advancing age. You can't take as much for granted, for example, and that tends to wake you up to life.

> *And when you don't want to do something, pretend you forgot. They never suspect.*

Thank You

—::—

Gratitude is not only the greatest of virtues, but the parent of all others.

  —Cicero

If you want to turn your life around, try thankfulness. It will change your life mightily.

  —Gerald Good

Being thankful, living life with an attitude of gratitude, is fundamental to happiness and generative to all other virtue.

I once knew a woman—OK, it was my mother—whose mantra in life was "We have so much to be thankful for!" As a boy hearing those words, I paid them scant attention, even occasionally thinking, "Well I don't know if we have that much to be thankful for! Life isn't all that great for me right now."

Over the years, these words have, obviously, stuck with me. Now I use them as my own mantra, even when life isn't too great. Their power comes from the effect the belief has on the person believing them. The belief affects all your responses to life.

Imagine saying "Thank you!" to everything that comes your way. The good stuff is easy: you get a new sweater at a great price; you bump into an old friend and have coffee; you hear a favorite piece of music; your kid surprises you with a profound and polite comment. The good stuff brings an easy gratitude.

But the "bad" stuff—a disturbing health diagnosis, financial pressure or failure, a bout of depression, an unfairness, a break-up, an accident—the list for human beings is endless. "Thank you" for that stuff? Well, think of the alternatives and consider their results: Anger? Upset? Screaming "Unfair!"? Resentment? Fighting? Where do they get you?

This isn't to say that we shouldn't try to avoid pain and suffering. It just means that, when the "bad stuff" inevitably happens and there's nothing you can do about it, try saying "Thank you" and see what happens.

Don't look at me! I didn't say I actually did it, just that it's a good idea!

Appreciation

— :: —

*Life can be seen through your eyes but it is not fully
appreciated until it is seen through your heart.*

—Mary Xavier

How gratifying to perceive that someone fully appreci-
ates what you have offered! It is indeed confirmation
that someone has seen not only "through your eyes,"
but "through your heart," as well. Thus I refer to this
meaning of "appreciated": *sensitive awareness; especially
recognition of values.*

I have a theory about appreciation. It is based on
a belief that appreciation is undervalued and misun-
derstood. My theory, bottom line, is that appreciation
is another way to understand spirituality, a subject of
interest to me both in theory and practice. It is also
my belief that everyone has a spirituality, religious or
not. Everyone "has" appreciation—that is, has sensitive
awareness and value recognition.

What do you appreciate? What are the things of
which you are sensitively aware, and what are the values

you recognize as your own? What gives you meaning? The answers to those questions comprise your spirituality.

Why is this at all important? Why bother to make these distinctions at all? Because, by making and recognizing your values and meanings, you embrace them with more awareness and identify more quickly whatever is antithetical to them. Thus you can live more authentically, more in line with what you consciously choose, rather than just accepting what happens to be fashionable or current.

Expressing appreciation is as important as embracing it. An unspoken "I appreciate it!" never brings to life its potential power, either to you and to the receiver. An undemonstrated "thank you!" lies fallow in your heart, and will never enrich the life of any other.

It is no accident that "appreciation" and "thankfulness" can be synonyms.

> *"Saying thank you is more than good manners. It is good spirituality" (Alfred Painter).*

Happiness I

— :: —

*To be happy is to be able to become aware of oneself
without fright.*

—Walter Benjamin

I find this statement remarkably insightful. Of all the
possible definitions or descriptions of happiness, I also
find it the most practical.

You are happy if and when you are able to become
self-aware. But the statement also implies that the most
common experience when attempting self-awareness is
fright.

It seems to me that the road to self-knowledge, and
thus to happiness, is traversed step by step rather than in
a single bound or with a mad dash to the finish. After
all, we can only stand so much truth at one time.

The first step is to accept a basic assumption
about happiness: It is not something that can be pur-
sued directly (*pace* the Declaration of Independence).
Happiness is the result of an integrated and meaning-
ful life. When you stop explicitly pursuing "happiness"

and focus on becoming more and more integrated and clearer and clearer on your meanings and values, happiness takes care of itself.

And while I'm still on my soapbox, the second step is to think a lot about what happiness is *for you*. Don't accept the smiley-faced, saccharine, painless, and unrealistic expectation that our culture often offers as a model and a goal ☺. Happiness is not an absence of problems and suffering. That's called fantasy.

Now, what about this fright factor? Self-awareness is always fearsome. It involves taking accurate stock of yourself and we are all terrified of what we will find when we do that. "The horror! The horror!" *Oh grow up and get over it!* In all probability, neither you nor I will take any prizes in being horrible. What we will see is simply a human person with all the foibles, all the graces, and all the challenges that go along with being human.

When you see the Smiley Face on the road, kill it! : (

Happiness II

— :: —

Perhaps the most important thing we can undertake toward the reduction of fear is to make it easier for people to accept themselves, to like themselves.

—Bonaro W. Overstreet

The last reflection encouraged you not to pursue happiness directly, but to see happiness in your own way. To do this, you must face the fears that come with self-awareness and see yourself as simply human.

Now comes the important part. Once you've seen yourself as a fully human being, love what you see! Easier said than done for some of us. You can go through all the logical arguments and reasons why you are indeed a lovable person; but if you don't believe it, all those rational arguments and reasons probably won't do much to change your heart. However, there is an answer to this too-common challenge. Find someone who loves you, or even just likes you. Then spend as much time as possible with them.

He came to us at a summer camp in New Hampshire already labeled as a problem and perhaps retarded or even autistic. The camp almost didn't accept him. He was twelve years old, emotionally flat, almost non-verbal, and generally unresponsive.

That is, until he met Cynthia, the camp cook. To make a summer-long story very short, Cynthia loved Jimmy to life. Soon, he was accepting the care and invitations to play from the other kids as well. He arrived never having experienced the creative love of adults; he left an emerging dynamo of life. All these years later, I still marvel and rejoice at the story. That entire camp community, led by Cynthia the cook, loved Jimmy into human life.

He was so starved for human affection and affirmation that, when it came to him in genuine form, he was more than ready and more than able to make up for the lost years. He learned through the real, concrete, expressed love of Cynthia and an accidental summer family that he was quite lovable indeed!

I like to think of Jimmy today perhaps loving his own kids—or someone else's, or anyone who needs it—into life.

Happiness is loving yourself.

Happiness III

— :: —

You will never be happy if you continue to search for what happiness consists of. You will never live if you are looking for the meaning of life.

—Albert Camus

Oh boy! I'm in trouble here.

I think I have spent a relatively large amount of time, compared to most people, thinking about happiness and what it is. I grew up hearing my father say that happiness is the most important thing in life. One of my regrets is that I never asked him just what happiness is, not that I would have expected him to expound much on the topic.

Most of us probably think of theoretical happiness in terms similar to those used in the Declaration of Independence: "Life, liberty, and the pursuit of happiness." Yes, Jefferson's word is "pursuit," an intense form of searching. So what is Camus, the existentialist French thinker who lived 150 years after Jefferson, going on about when he says searching for happiness won't make you happy? Well, for starters, Jefferson was a politician; Camus a philosopher.

Maybe happiness happens as a result of something much more basic than either searching for or acquiring it. Happiness is, rather, the specific quality of the accumulated moments of your life. It is a by-product, if you will. Fill this moment with meaning and the life takes care of itself.

Come to think of it, I believe that is what my father meant when he said, "Happiness is the most important thing." Having lived through the 20th century with all its turbulence, violence, and changes, his style was simply to fill his moments with what the moment, the hour, and the day brought him—quietly, gently.

I started this reflection saying that I was in trouble because I have not taken Camus' advice to heart. I *like* to think about what happiness is! However, I believe Camus is right. Searching for any precisely defined happiness has never added to my experienced feelings of being happy. Analyzing the ultimate meaning of life—always a futile endeavor—has added no experience of joy to my life.

On the other hand, a moment of contemplating my father's dignified life does indeed bring me much happiness and a moment of joy.

My resolution: Just focus on the moments, David. The life will take care of itself. Will you join me?

CHAPTER 2

Creativity and Art

— :: —

Metaphor

God is a metaphor for that which transcends all levels of intellectual thought. It's as simple as that.

—Joseph Campbell

As a schoolboy, I learned that a metaphor is a figure of speech. It is similar to a simile, but it doesn't use the words "like" or "as." *She was as pretty as a picture* is a simile. *She was a tiger in a cage* is a metaphor. What I didn't know as a schoolboy is that we can hardly speak without metaphors. Everything can be a metaphor. Why not begin at the top as Joseph Campbell, a lion of a man, did.

Simply put, a metaphor is a word or phrase that literally denotes one kind of object or idea but is used in place of another to suggest a likeness. It's an incredible short-cut to meaning: Contrast *He was drowning in money* to *He had so much money that it was threatening his well-being* or any other non-metaphoric expression of the same idea.

Metaphors are the gold of human communication. They fly us to the summits of truth. That is, they take us quickly to levels of meaning and nuance that are unavailable without them.

Just try life without metaphors. It certainly wouldn't be a bowl of cherries; more likely a vale of tears.

So my point here is to make you aware of the metaphors you use. They can tell you a lot about yourself.

What do you call your spouse? What metaphor do you use? Honey? Sweetie? She-who-must-be-obeyed? Mr. Fix-it? How do you describe your boss? Amazon? Monster? Commander-in-chief? Mr. Cold Heart? Ms. Perfect? Is your job the salt mines? Is your commute an agony? Are your co-workers robots?

The metaphors you use not only reveal your attitudes; they *create* them. The more you repeat the metaphor, the more accurate it is likely to become. So if you notice your boss becoming more and more domineering and demanding, maybe "slave-driver" is not the best way to refer to her.

> *"Unless you are educated in metaphor, you are not safe to be let loose in the world" (Robert Frost).*

Take a Shot

— :: —

You miss 100 percent of the shots you never take.

—Wayne Gretzky

There are two extremes to avoid when you are forming an opinion of yourself: Over-inflation *(I can do anything)* and under-inflation *(I can't do nothin').*

Easy to say; hard to live. When should you just give up and let it go, and when should you go all out and give it your best shot?

I remember so clearly about twenty years ago when it first occurred to me to write. I was a family therapist. Something came up in the course of therapy with a particular client that made me think, "I bet a lot of people have this same challenge. Maybe I can write about it."

My next thoughts went something like this: "But I have always had a hard time writing, from term papers in high school to my dissertation in graduate school, which almost did me in. There are already too many things published; you're not going to add anything new. Fuggedaboudit."

That was the moment of truth: Forget it or try something? I can do anything, or I can't do nothin'? My response was somewhere in the middle. I wrote a brief article, which I gave to my client. But then I didn't know what to do with it, how to get it published. So I expanded it, printed it myself, and soon wearied of trying to sell it (very few sold) or give it away (too expensive). Finally, I sent my little booklet off to three publishers. To my amazement, one of them accepted it.

From serious self-doubt to moderate success—because I took the shot. Over the years, I have also had many lost opportunities. What else might have been, had I taken the shot? Now I'll never know.

The words of Gretzky, Canadian hockey legend, ring true. I picture him, a blur of rhythm and power on the ice, always looking, alert, hoping never to miss his chance, his shot at a goal—and I make a quiet resolve.

And you? Overconfident? Chicken? Need to take a shot at something?

Seeing

— :: —

Art does not reproduce what we see; rather, it makes us see.

—Paul Klee

In addition to comfortable shoes and a program, I invite you to consider taking something else along as you enter an art museum or gallery: your assumptions.

➤ Do you want to be impressed? *Oh, look, there's a Picasso! I've never seen so many Monets!*

➤ Does everything you look at in the museum fall into two categories? *I like it. I don't like it.*

➤ Do you come simply as a respite from a too-busy life? *This is such a peaceful and quiet place to be. Oh, yes, there is art here.*

➤ Do you come as one ignorant of art? *What do I know about art? Nothing, really, so I'll just wander and look at it and leave . . . unchanged.*

➤ Are you especially impressed by the technical skills of the artist? *How did she ever manage to get that effect?*

➤ Do you come to judge? *I love that! I hate that! My two-year-old could do that!*

➤ Do you come to art to learn something from the artist?

I've had my time with all of these assumptions and probably others as well. And I would guess you have, too. It's the last assumption I try to choose consciously, as often as I can manage it. But it's not easy.

The question that Paul Klee (Swiss–German of the early 20th century) enjoins us to ask is so direct, so accurate, so clean: What is the artist trying to make me see? It's almost always a good question to bring to any piece of art. The artist wants to change you. Will you change? The artist wants to communicate something to you. Will you hear?

> *The next time you encounter art, ask: "What do you want me to see, feel, understand?"*

Enduring Art

— :: —

All passes, Art alone
Enduring stays to us;
The Bust outlasts the throne,
The Coin, Tiberius.

　　　—Henry Austin Dobson

I am strongly attracted to this 19th-century poem by the English poet Dobson. Only art endures, all the rest passes away. (I think there is some schlock that has endured, as well.)

But it's the second half of the poem that has the bite: the bust of the king may well reside in the museum centuries after the king is forgotten. The coin with the image of Tiberius has lasted 1,970 years beyond the death of the emperor and will doubtless go on indefinitely. Dust to dust. *Sic transit gloria mundi.*

So consider this: Everything in your home will likely outlast you. You'll be gone, and all that stuff will still be around. Somebody will inherit it, buy it, sell it, steal it, otherwise acquire it, throw it away, or give it away. Rooms of stuff. Your stuff.

Doesn't that seem to put some vaguely moral obligation on all of us to acquire only what is beautiful, pleasing, artistic? Or at least the more beautiful of our available choices? (Well, that's useless, I suppose, since one person's *beauty* is another's *ugly!* But still . . .)

How do you surround yourself with art? Or more to the point, *do* you surround yourself with art, with an eye to making the spaces in your life beautiful, appealing, artistic? It does influence how you feel when you are in those spaces and how others feel when you invite them in. No need for extravagance or great expense. Just art.

> *Look at your spaces with the eye of the artist that you are.*

Be Cool

— :: —

In music one must think with the heart and feel with the brain.

—George Szell

George Szell has been familiar to me since childhood. He was the Hungarian-born conductor of the Cleveland Symphony Orchestra from 1946 to 1970. Gifted and demanding, he is credited with bringing the orchestra from obscurity to the peak of world-wide symphonic performance.

Frequently, during my high school years in Cleveland—and unlikely for a teenager—I sat alone in a crowd at Severance Hall simply enjoying his performances, which are now seen as classically brilliant. For me, these performances were simply a haven, a refuge from the messy demands of adolescence. I thought it was really cool.

So I was especially struck by Szell's compelling statement above. It is counter-intuitive and thought-provoking: *thinking* with your heart and *feeling* with your brain. Just how does that work? Szell seems, in switching the feeling and thinking functions, to under-cut the essential energy of both. Both the thinking and the feeling are weakened, so to speak, not enhanced. In the end, what remains for me is coolness. Indeed, critics sometimes complained that Szell's performances were brilliant, but somewhat stiff, overly-rehearsed, and cool.

Maybe the best way to understand the thinking heart and feeling brain is to see them as very deep feeling that is kept under control or expressed in exactness and order, rather than in any kind of an emotional, messy way. Coolness rather than heat. Yes, I think that's it. I think Szell would have liked that interpretation.

And your thinking heart and feeling brain? Are there any situations in your life that demand a lot of emotional energy and conviction, but in which you cannot risk too much exposure and attention?

Try it with music.

Writing to Learn

— :: —

I do not sit down at my desk to put into verse something that is already clear in my mind. If it were clear in my mind, I should have no incentive or need to write about it. We do not write to be understood; we write to understand.

—Cecil Day-Lewis

I won't claim that this is always true for me, but most often it is. When you write about something, by the very nature of the act of writing, you must think about it, sort it out, try to make sense of it, awaken to its realities.

The first serious piece of writing I attempted was an assignment in senior English in high school. To pass the course, we had to research and write what seemed at the time a very long term paper (I think it was about fifty pages). It was very difficult for me. Fifty pages seemed beyond my capabilities. I had no idea what it was like to write that much. My topic: *The Byzantine Influence on the Painting of El Greco.* (Who was I kidding?) Yet, it was way back then that I realized that, once you get into your subject, it sort of takes over. And you learn. It was a poorly written paper (I think I got a "C"), but it was a start.

It is said that the famous Russian playwright Anton Chekhov once responded to a reader that it was not the writer's responsibility to solve problems, but to state the problems accurately. That accurate statement expresses much working through, much contemplation, and often much internal battling.

When I first started a short but enjoyable time as a high school teacher, I was asked to teach first-year Spanish. "But I don't know Spanish that well," I replied to the principal. "Teaching is the best way to learn," he replied. Thanks.

The same for writing. If you want to understand and learn something, begin to write about it. Don't worry about being published. Simply pick a subject in which you have interest and begin to write about it— perhaps just in an email to a friend, or a letter to the editor.

Begin to write something. No excuses. Just begin.

Obsession

— :: —

Our town is an ordinary town, just like any other.

—Thornton Wilder

One of my obsessions, one I'm willing to acknowledge, is Thornton Wilder's 1938 play, *Our Town*. On one occasion, I drove 350 miles to see a production of it; on another, 500 miles. If it's performed anywhere near my home, I am in the audience. If it's presented on TV, I watch. I read it almost yearly. As I am writing this, I have a ticket for a performance in three months in Oregon. As I said, I'm obsessed.

I first read the play as a fifteen-year-old in my sophomore year of high school in American Literature class. You probably did too. Somehow, that play got to me in a way that was deep and permanent. That often happens to us in those early adolescent years—something makes so strong an impression that it lasts a lifetime.

Some critics don't think this is a really great play; perhaps it isn't. No matter; it's mine in a very intimate way and, to me, it is great.

It's a harmless obsession. It's mildly annoying to my partner (*Please don't ask me to sit through that again!*) and mysterious to my friends (*Yes, I remember reading it in school. You've seen it how many times? Why?*) I have no answer to these comments and queries; there is no answer. *Our Town* is part of me in a way that is permanent and mysterious. I love it.

Here's another admission: every time I see it, I cry. It's not really anything I can control and it's often embarrassing to me and to anyone with me. There are several points at which tears may well up, but the one sure spot is during Emily's monologue in the third act: "Oh, Mama, just look at me one minute as though you really saw me."

What is your obsession? A place? A book? A poem? Some other written work? An occasion? A person or people? An age or period of life? Shapes or designs? A piece of art? A color? Or . . . ?

> *Awaken to what is in you personally, deeply, permanently.*

Reclaiming Awareness

— :: —

The only thing that can save the world is the reclaiming of the awareness of the world. That's what poetry does.

—Allen Ginsberg

Poetry does it—as do many of the other arts and insights human beings are able to create. The strong implication in the Beat poet's comment is that, if you become aware, really aware, of the world as it is, the saving of it will take care of itself.

Imagine the power of the statement for a moment. If you truly see the world in all its wonder and grandeur, power and might, beauty and immensity, you will change your life. The very realization would simply demand it. Poetry and art lead you more deeply into that realization.

So just how aware of the world are you? Am I? Well, I can only say that I think, I hope, that I am on the way, traveling on the road to greater awareness. Falling off track, losing my way, and getting confused are all part of the journey. There is no end in sight. Nor will there ever be, I think. The only goal is to keep getting back on the road.

What helps? Poetry and art! That's what they are about. They keep you on the track of awareness, of mindfulness, of seeing the world in any of its zillions of manifestations. Art and poetry often and simply say to the beholder, Look! Feel! Behold! Consider! Contemplate!—or maybe just Wow! For example, here is "Oceans" by Spanish poet Juan Ramon Jimenez (1881–1958).

I have a feeling that my boat
has struck, down there in the depths,
against a great thing.
And nothing
happens! Nothing . . . Silence . . . Waves . . .

—Nothing happens? Or has everything happened,
and are we standing now, quietly, in the new life?

> *. . . or has everything happened?*

Imagination

— :: —

*No problem can be solved from the same level of
consciousness that created it.*

—Albert Einstein

I like to think that a corollary to Einstein's famous
statement is: You can't do or become anything new unless you can first imagine it. Maybe they are related—
achieving a new level of consciousness and imagining
yourself in a new way of being in the world. Or maybe
they are almost the same thing—bringing your consciousness to a new level of seeing, of understanding,
of knowing.

I'll never forget, as a boy, trying to imagine eternity.
I doggedly tried to imagine "going on forever with no
end." But I never reached the end of my imagining.
I just got tired or bored and gave it up. I can't imagine eternity, I thought, so I can't be eternal. If you can
imagine eternity, then you must be eternal.

On a more down-to-earth note, I remember a conversation with a friend who is a fiction writer. I said

something like, "I just can't imagine writing fiction." Without missing a beat, she replied, "Well, then you can't." Right.

As you try to solve problems:

➤ Spend time in your imagination. Let it go wild—that is, let it go to places that your thinking mind may label as ridiculous, nonsensical, or impossible.

➤ Close your eyes, sit back quietly, and visualize that you have solved your problem. Then work backward from the solution.

➤ As you are imagining, pay very close attention to the images that come to you and that form in your mind's eye without invitation. They will invariably offer something useful. You may "see" a freight train or a light bulb or a tulip. Welcome it; don't dismiss it. Talk to it; listen to it.

What can you imagine today?

Conversation

—::—

To talk with someone,
ask a question first,
then—listen.

—Antonio Machado

Who are you?

Whatever answer springs from the riches of your inner life can now warm the hearts of all who are open.

Me! Please come in.

What is deep in my soul now has new life in yours.

The responses may fill an evening or a lifetime; they may provide riches enough for a new world.

To talk with another is amazing intimacy. The miracle of language leaps the abyss between human hearts.

Say more; we've just begun.

Wonderful tales.

What stories!

They remind me of what I thought forgotten. But here it is, new again, ready to surprise and delight.

Now I'll tell you a story; it's so simple.

It takes your breath away?

That little yarn from so long ago?

Oh, yes, of course! It brings another time—and another story that you will tell me.

I hear the voices of the world. I listen to songs of the nations. I feel the embrace of the gods.

I am wrapped in your telling.

You live in my story.

I am drawn inside of your tale.

I guess that means we love each other.

Amen.

Realism

— :: —

Nothing is less real than realism. Details are confusing.
It is only by selection, by elimination, by emphasis that
we get to the real meaning of things.

—Georgia O'Keeffe

O'Keeffe is giving us a good way to begin to understand "abstract" art, or perhaps more accurately, "non-
representational" art. It's a matter of language, ultimately,
but I believe that "abstract" refers to art that makes no attempt to represent some external reality (think Mondrian,
Pollock, Kandinsky) and that "non-representational" art
like O'Keeffe's synthesizes abstraction and representation.

Who, after looking at an O'Keeffe painting of the
sky or a flower, can see them in the same way again?
Why does she not simply "paint what she sees there?"
She does! She simply does not see what I see!

She sees abstractly. She tells us why in her words
above. "By selection, by elimination, by emphasis," she
gets to the real meaning—the essence, the heart.

The proof of the method is in her results.

I wonder if I can do that in other areas? Can I abstract you? Can I not pay any attention to your "confusing details" and simply see the essence of who you are? Can I respond to that? Celebrate that?

Can I do that with challenges? Can I identify the unimportant elements that give me no unique information? Can I let them go and focus on what truly creates the problem?

Is it possible to synthesize abstraction and representation with life itself? Can I learn an attitude that recognizes what is frivolous, non-lasting, even evil, while homing in on universal values and meanings?

Ultimately, I wonder if I can do that with myself? Reality, and the practice of realism that embraces it, is a powerful force. These eyes are trained by the ages to "see things as they are!"

. . . or so I've been told.

The Price of Art

—::—

*Art is unthinkable without risk and spiritual
self-sacrifice.*

—Boris Pasternak

Well, it seems to me that there is a lot of what is offered as
"art" that has not been born of risk and self-sacrifice.

Let's assume that Pasternak, Russian writer (*Dr.
Zhivago*) and poet, means the best art, true art. He certainly can include his own writing. He was awarded the
Nobel Prize for literature, which he rejected, probably
out of fear of serious reprisal by the Communist regime
and loss of citizenship if he left his country to receive
it. Risk and spiritual self-sacrifice shine throughout his
varied and creative life.

For me, the appreciation of art is, without exception, enhanced when I know something about the
nature of the person who produced it. Art is always a
production of the soul, of the lived life of the artist, no
matter what he or she paints or sculpts. It shines forth in
every detail. The challenge—and it's a worthy challenge
indeed!—is to see it.

Look into the lives of artists whose work attracts you. Do you like van Gogh's? You have an amazing tale to learn. Are you attracted to Georgia O'Keeffe? What a ride she had! How about the sculptor Rodin? Or Michelangelo? When you enter the tales and details of their lives you personalize their work and embrace it anew.

Or what about the guy down the street who paints on weekends? He is as capable of risk and self-sacrifice as anyone. Look for it. Or your child's art teacher, who spends most of her time teaching and gives only the hours she can spare to her beloved painting? Her risks and sacrifice may be astounding, unimaginable. She may embody Pasternak's words, deeming "unthinkable" anything that does not expose her soul and risk, among other things, rejection and ridicule. Watch for it.

> *The more you know the artist, the more you know the art.*

CHAPTER 3

Emotional Life

— :: —

Scream

Sometimes a scream is better than a thesis.

—Ralph Waldo Emerson

It certainly is better at getting your attention.

I've felt like screaming once or twice in my time—at least metaphorically. I wonder, however, if I have ever really screamed out loud, in public? I don't think so; at least I can't remember doing it. Oh, maybe at a ballgame where my screams were absorbed in the crowd's; but that doesn't count. It would be very unlike me to scream out loud in public. But there have certainly been times when I wished I could.

People who are members of cultural minorities tend to scream. Sometimes it's the only way to get attention. I believe Screamers have done more than we know to advance the causes of the oppressed.

I am making a resolve that, the next time a scream is called for, I will do my best to let it out. It scares me just thinking about it.

And you? What about you and screaming? Too brash? Too uncivilized? Too lower class? Too . . . what? Think about it a moment.

I think of the movie *Network* (1976), in which the character Howard Beale eventually gets throngs of people to yell out publicly to the world: "I'm mad as hell and I'm not going to take it anymore!" It struck a national chord at the time and you still hear the phrase from time to time. Maybe we should hear it more.

Is this a scream that carries a sentiment you can relate to? No? Yes? Why? Why not?

Is it more your style to create a carefully crafted and thought-out thesis, as in Emerson's example? It certainly is for me. I can't help thinking that screaming really does no good—ultimately. It often offends and moves the cause backward, not forward.

Maybe. But in the long run—maybe not.

If you had to, what would you scream to the world?

Sadness I

— :: —

People need to be sad as much as they need to be happy.
We're made that way. The Lord knows why.

—Louise Dean

There was a period in my life, not all that long ago, when I existed in a very sad state. Not sad as in depressed or deplorable or regrettable or of little worth, but sad as in feeling grief over loss.

I have written on the benefit, especially for men, of getting in touch with their feeling life and expressing whatever they feel in a healthy and clear way. I don't always practice what I preach. I am, however, a good example of why writers often write about what they need to learn.

It is often difficult for me to express feelings of sadness directly and openly. Why, I ask myself? What's so difficult about letting the world know you're sad? The first reason that comes to mind is that "no one likes a sad sack." It's true. Given the social values of our culture, sadness is an unwelcome visitor to the party. It puts a "damper" on everything; it's a "downer."

At the same time, as Irish writer Dean says, it's part of our nature. "We're made that way."

So here's the deal: Wake up and allow yourself—even more, encourage yourself—simply to be sad if that's what you're feeling. You can certainly become a bit more creative with your feelings and more imaginative in their expression, but however you do it, feel the sadness that comes to literally all of us from grief over our continuing losses. Not to feel and express sadness is to keep that energy captive in your soul, where it eventually turns on you and does damage. Do you think that all physical symptoms always have physical causes?

An encouragement: The best way—really the only way—to fulfill the feeling of sadness is to express it to the world in some way.

What sadness do you have waiting for expression?

Sadness II

— :: —

Life is an onion and one peels it crying.

— French proverb

During the same period of sadness I mentioned in the previous reflection, I decided to seek some help. On the recommendation of a friend and colleague, I sought the services of a Jesuit spiritual advisor. He was a seasoned old Jesuit who had learned a lot about human nature in his many years of ministry. He was a man of few words, not easily misled.

We met six times. At the first session, I told him about myself and my recent feelings of depression— that's what I called it at the time, not sadness. (Indeed, it was he who helped me see the truth.) During the next five sessions, I went to his little office, sat down in a straight-backed chair, and did the same thing every time: I cried.

I find it a bit embarrassing to say it here. It's often not easy for a man to cry and even harder for him to admit it. But the truth is that's what I did. I sat down and began to cry. As I recall, I cried through almost all of the last five sessions. In between tears, we shared a lot of silence, and very few words.

I write of this for two reasons. First, I realized from that experience the immense amount of grief and sadness we all carry and the very good reasons we have to cry about it. I was not depressed. I was massively sad over the losses of my life (nothing extraordinary, just human losses), as well as the losses of our common national, international, and simply human lives. We all lose, all the time—and the grief piles up. It needs to find expression.

I also write about it to show the simple process by which sadness can be facilitated and expressed. The Jesuit said very little—no great insights, no spiritual revelations, nor any attempt at them. But he showed by his attentive and understanding presence that I was expressing something human and normal and acceptable. He got it.

From time to time, I stammered, "I don't know why I'm doing this; I feel sort of stupid." He simply answered, "That's fine, just let it happen and don't worry about why. It's there and it needs to come out."

So I encourage you to find good ways (not necessarily crying, but maybe) to identify and express your grief over loss. And find ways to allow or encourage or facilitate others to do the same.

You'll feel better. I did.

Sincere Ignorance

— :: —

Nothing in the world is more dangerous than sincere ignorance and conscientious stupidity.

—Martin Luther King, Jr.

It's a deadly mix, ignorance and stupidity. Horrible things result. The civil rights leader knew personally whereof he spoke; he felt the results in his own life and especially in his violent death.

All I have to do is look into my own history, to those times when I was sure my course of action was the right one. I was positive it was right, perhaps especially because I saw myself as so completely sincere!

But I wasn't right. That soon became clear to everyone, including me. I guess that I am not alone in my experience of being both ignorant and stupid. The danger occurs when, to put it bluntly, you don't have the information necessary for the situation at hand (ignorant) and at the same time you act on the basis of that ignorance (stupid). It's the perfect recipe for disaster.

When I was studying moral theology, I learned to make a distinction between invincible and vincible ignorance. The former is literally "not conquerable"—you can't reasonably be expected to have some kinds of knowledge and information. (Sometimes you don't know something and there's no good reason why you should know it.) The latter occurs when you don't know something and there are solid reasons why you should know it.

The combination against which King warns seems to involve invincible (his word is "sincere") ignorance. In other words, he's talking about the good people of the world—you and me, not the scoundrels. He's talking to people who genuinely believe they are doing what is absolutely right and for the good of all. They have sincere hearts. They are the dangerous ones. Or should I say *we* are the dangerous ones? We've all been there—which means we can all be there again.

How can this be overcome? With prayer and fasting. By that I mean with extreme vigilance and self-scrutiny of our causes, with relentless examination of our motives and the available facts. And even then, we must always leave room for change, for growth, and for insight.

> *Does this mean I have to look again at my deepest convictions?*

Letting Go

—⠂⠂—

Think about any attachments that are depleting your emotional reserves. Consider letting them go.

—Oprah Winfrey

The depletion of our "emotional reserves" is something we really cannot afford these days. Our reserves are depleted enough, and every day brings new demands for emotional energy and presence.

Somewhere along the way, I remember hearing the following story. Two Buddhist monks were on a long journey. One morning, they came to a wide but shallow river with no bridge or ferry. Standing on the bank, they observed another traveler, a beautiful young woman who was much distressed. She told them that she was not strong enough to cross the river alone. One of the monks immediately offered to carry her across. She accepted his offer. When they all reached the other side, the young woman expressed her gratitude and went on her way, as did the two monks.

That evening, the monk who had not carried the lady said, "You were very wrong and immoral to put yourself in such an intimate situation with that beautiful young woman." His companion thought a moment and said, "I carried the woman across the river and let go of her on the other side. It seems you have been carrying her all day."

Consider what attachments you carry. Become awake to any unnecessary anxieties, worries, memories, angers, guilty feelings, sorrows, and frustrations that are depleting your emotional reserves.

Right now, as you are reading this, make a fist with one hand. "Place" inside that fist every attachment that is depleting you, that is weighing you down, that is a burden to you, that is weakening you, and that you don't want to carry. Now simply make your fist into an open hand and let go. Let this simple gesture become for you a symbol of letting go of those attachments that deplete you.

Use this "Letting Go" ritual often.

Smart with Feelings

—::—

Researchers have found that even more than IQ, your emotional awareness and abilities to handle feelings will determine your success and happiness in all walks of life, including family relationships.

—John Gottman

This is one of the relatively new and important bits of reality that has emerged from the shadows and joined the immense flow of information in our age. I say "relatively new" because, although the information has been around for ages, it has been brought to consciousness and made easily accessible in the last ten years. Its importance, while not earthshaking, has a revolutionary feel to it.

According to Gottman, how you deal with your emotions has as much, if not more, effect on your eventual happiness and success as your native intelligence, your IQ. If we believe that, then we should begin, as a culture, to include the emotions in a specific (perhaps even curricular) way in our systems of education. As it is now, our emotional side gets trained and developed— or not—willy-nilly.

This is a subject close to my heart. I have written about it in a book especially for men. (*Nothing's Wrong: A Man's Guide to Managing His Feelings*) I have seen, and continue to see, so many people—women as well as men, teenagers to grandparents—who often stumble as they try to "make it" in life and have no clue why they don't succeed. So many people in our Western world can not recognize an emotion even if they trip over it. And, if they do recognize it for what it is, they do not know how to "handle" it intelligently, wisely, and appropriately.

Again, this has momentous implications for educators and parents, and for anyone who cares about the complete development of the individual.

We now know for certain what many ancient civilizations knew instinctively: being intelligent includes being smart with your feelings. If this idea is new to you, begin exploring it by reading Daniel Goleman's *Emotional Intelligence.* If this idea is not new to you, what can you do to help those you love and those around you to wake up to this significant and far-reaching insight into human development?

Being smart with your feelings. What a concept!

Personal Fear

— :: —

The best remedy for those who are afraid, lonely or unhappy is to go outside, somewhere where they can be quiet, alone with the heavens, nature and God. Because only then does one feel that all is as it should be and that God wishes to see people happy, amidst the simple beauty of nature.

—Anne Frank

I will always remember an experience I had when I lived and worked in Idaho. I had made arrangements to interview a twenty-year-old student from New Jersey, Jacob, who had an opportunity to come study and work in Idaho. He arrived in Boise in the evening and, the next morning, a colleague and I decided to show him a bit of our state. We drove north toward Idaho City, a "ghost town" and national wilderness area. During the drive, Jacob became more and more quiet and non-responsive. I didn't pay much attention, but remember wondering why. We brought along some sandwiches and, at a quiet place along the river, stopped for lunch.

By the time we stopped, Jacob could hardly speak. We were concerned for his well-being and asked what could we do to help. "I want to go back," was all he could stammer. So we immediately did. As we arrived back in the city, he was finally able, somewhat, to articulate his fear. "There was nothing there! What if I got sick? There is no one around!" He went on and on about how afraid he was to be in such an isolated place—something that he had never experienced before. His fear literally became paralysis. He could not speak or move; he never got out of the car.

Needless to say, he never came to Idaho. Clearly, young Anne Frank's comment (where did she get such wisdom?!) about being alone in nature is, sadly, lost on people like Jacob.

Do you know someone like Jacob? Do you know young people who have never known isolation in the wilderness, or even experienced semi-tame nature? Who have no experience of being "alone with the heavens?" Find a way to take them into nature and guide them to see it as Anne Frank did. Help them to "go outside, somewhere where they can be quiet," to "feel that all is as it should be" and know that "God wishes to see people happy, amidst the simple beauty of nature."

And do it for yourself, too.

Insecurity

— :: —

*No bum that can't speak poifect English oughta stay in
this country . . . oughta be de-exported the hell outta
here!*

—Archie Bunker

All in the Family (TV comedy 1971–1979) gave us one
of television's most memorable characters in Archie
Bunker. A more bigoted and ignorant loud-mouthed
know-it-all you could not find. And yet, perhaps to the
surprise of the show's writers, Archie became something of a national hero. The viewing audience loved
him. It seems Middle America identified with him,
shared many of his views, and overlooked in him the
same attitudes and prejudices they wanted to overlook
in themselves. Archie was, after all is said and done,
loveable—wasn't he?

Archie was not really bad, not really evil or ill-
meaning, just, just . . . what? For one thing, he was very
funny. He was, I believe, a brilliantly conceived and presented comic character. Even more so because, underneath, you could tell that he had a soft heart. So if you're

bigoted and ignorant and loudly opinionated, but at the same time funny and have a basically good heart, you're . . . what?

Afraid. Lacking self-confidence.

Bluster and loud-mouthed energy often cover fear. Archie's chief antagonist was his son-in-law, whom he called Meathead (his wife was Dingbat). It is no accident that Meathead was a graduate student attending a "liberal" university, engaged in the intellectual life and conversant with social conditions. He was Archie's perfect foil.

But the fact is that we all loved Archie—everyone, no matter where they fell on the left-right political spectrum. That's because most of us could identify with him. Which of us never blustered in some way to hide our weakness? Or took the easy way out by mocking an idea rather than responding to it? Or made up clever names for people as a way to show disdain? Humor is an effective and common way to cover fear.

Take a look underneath your humor.

CHAPTER 4

Systems: Secular and Sacred

— :: —

Adulation

I'm nobody! Who are you?
Are you nobody, too?

—Emily Dickinson

Our country has developed, and perhaps even perfected, the cult of celebrity. The rich and the famous have a powerful influence on almost every aspect of our culture, whether or not they have insight, knowledge, or even care.

Movie stars and athletes, it seems, are raised to special heights of celebrity. They are generally attractive and rich, and often lead flamboyant and extravagant lives. Often, they are good at what they do—but not always. Sometimes they are charismatic as well.

Does the bestowal of celebrity say more about the bestowers than about the receivers? Yes, I think it says much about "us," and not as much about "them."

Projection is the psychological term. Vicarious living, wishful thinking, fantasy, and pipe dreams are other terms. In some way, we want to be like celebrities, so we celebrate them. *At least someone has achieved "greatness" even if we can't*, we tell ourselves.

Somehow, we don't seem to consider that the very celebrity we bestow also robs the celebs of freedom and normalcy in their lives. Just think of Princess Diana. Celebrities live in an unreal hothouse environment; they commonly become quite odd, and so it seems from what we read, not very happy.

And, truth be told, a few celebrities rise to the occasion and become genuinely integrated people of remarkable character.

For my money, Emily Dickinson (quoted above) had it right. She became a celebrity long after she was gone. Her life was quiet and peaceful, just the way she wanted it. No *paparazzi* in Amherst, Massachusetts in the middle of the 19th century.

Bestowing celebrity on those we admire and respect is not bad; it is a most human trait. Make your own list of celebrities. Whom do you want to celebrate? And just how will you do that? Write down the names of a few people you appreciate and want to celebrate—living or dead, famous or infamous, acquaintance or stranger, local or foreign. Then celebrate them.

> *For encouragement, read Dickinson's entire poem.*
> *She captured the idea, with joy, in eight lines.*

Crazy Systems

— :: —

Modern man is even more sick in normality than in the asylum.

—C. G. Jung

Carl Jung (1875–1961), eminent Swiss physician and psychiatrist, lived in a time when systems were better off than they are now. They hadn't yet been degraded as they are today, and thus his insight is even more accurate a century later.

To paraphrase Jung's concept, we now experience "institutionalized craziness" in the systems of our society. By "systems," I mean the organizations and institutions we create in our schools, branches of government, churches, military, and so on.

> Your straight-A-daughter's school tells you she cannot advance to ninth grade because she was unable to attend a mandated assembly on safety because of her music recital. Sorry.

> Your parish church tells you that you cannot play a recording of Beethoven's Fifth Symphony at your father's

funeral because church rules prohibit "secular" music during its "sacred" liturgy. So sorry.

➤ You can't vote in an election because you need to fill out a registration form, but they have changed the form and it is not printed yet. Sorry.

As soon as something becomes institutionalized, it begins to travel down the road to insanity. We all have our stories, I'm sure. Something that is obviously senseless can nevertheless become standard practice because the institution has its rules. It seems to be a common progression throughout all of human history.

So the question, as I see it, is two-fold. How can I change the institutions of which I am a member, by making them flexible, spontaneous, sane, and kind? Stand up for what you know is healthy, fair, and common sense. And am I giving institutions more respect and obedience than they deserve or even than is good for them? Question authority.

If you're not skeptical about institutions, you're asleep. The only sane 21st-century attitude toward institutions is mistrust, doubt, and challenge. This is a tough one, because it often seems so hopeless.

You have to start somewhere. Where will you start?

Certainty and Doubt

— :: —

*The whole problem with the world is that fools and
fanatics are always so certain of themselves, but wiser
people so full of doubts.*

—Bertrand Russell

When it comes to competition or argument, those who
doubt most often loose; those who are certain win. It's
the nature of the two contrasting points of view. I'll
admit up front that I find it difficult to be objective
here. I know that roughly half the world would change
Russell's statement to read: Fools and fanatics are full of
doubts and the wise are certain. I don't believe it. My
experience, at least, does not back that up.

To oversimplify positively, progressive-thinking people see all sides of a question in an attempt to get it
right. Conservative-thinking people hold to one answer
as the truth. To grossly oversimplify negatively, liberals
are wishy-washy, conservatives are fixated. Progressives
make lots of mistakes because they try lots of different things; conservatives avoid mistakes by doing everything possible to prevent change—including correcting

existing mistakes. Both sides have their challenges and their weaknesses. What to do?

As a self-proclaimed progressive, I want to say to conservatives: *Don't be afraid! Acknowledge the obvious truth that there are many ways to look at the world, not just one!* And they probably want to say to me . . . well, I'm not sure what they want to say. Maybe something like: *Don't be so arrogant. How do you know our way is not indeed the right way?* Well, that's just the point, I don't! But, I want to add, neither do you! Wake up!

Problems get solved when there is free discussion, sharing of differing points of view, mutual respect, and honest doubt. There's nothing new here. Oh, the frustration!

Of course, I know that these fundamental differences will not change. I believe, however, that, somehow, we must grow—*all of us*—in our willingness and ability to minimize our differences, to allow for peaceful consensus, and to listen to each other more attentively and without threat. Our lives depend on it.

Find a way to begin–today.

Trickle-down Values

— :: —

A leader leads by example, whether he intends to or not.

—American Proverb

You may be reading this just before, just after, or a long way from a presidential election. Whichever the case, I humbly suggest that you keep this proverb in mind when you vote. Invariably, what is important to the person at the top quickly becomes important to the rest of the crowd. I believe this is especially true when dealing with values, which are difficult to analyze.

I'm sure you've seen this clearly in politics. But you need look no further than your place of work and your boss for examples.

What does your boss value? Fairness and kindness? The bottom line and money? Family life and children? Social justice and human rights? Self-adulation and power? Looks and social status? Whatever values people in power embrace soon become the popular ones, the "right" ones. It is inevitable.

So when you vote for a president, or choose anyone for a leadership role, this is an important element to keep in mind: Soon, this person's values will be the country's (the city's, the school's, the organization's). They will trickle down, as surely as water seeks its own level.

My own experience with this idea is not so high-level and not so great. I was the head of a small organization. And, sure enough, my values trickled down. At that particular time, my values, from my present perspective, were skewed. I was more interested in playing racquetball than I was in engaging with the thorny challenges of the organization; more interested in developing friendships than in administration.

When I look back now, I see my organization was friendly, but adrift—badly in need of a strong hand, of a leader with the values of decisiveness and order, the values that come from leading, possibly at the price of popularity.

> *Be aware that you, and all of us, are the recipients of trickle-down values. And be aware that your values trickle down on others.*

Do Something

—::—

The mania started with insomnia and not eating and being driven, driven to find an apartment, driven to see everybody, driven to do New York, driven to never shut up.

—Patty Duke

We live in a manic culture. That is to say, the world around us—our institutions and organizations, our private and our public lives—are all driven to do more and more, faster and faster.

Stop a moment and consider the implication of those last words: "More and more, faster and faster." The two imperatives are not mutually supportive. Combining them must end, inevitably, in disaster. Something has to give. Unfortunately, what usually "gives" is the people involved—you and I. We can respond to this mania either intentionally and healthily, or unintentionally and unhealthily. Your choice. To be healthy, you *have* to respond. You *must* do something. We all must. Otherwise, you become a passive victim—you get sick, have an "accident," mess up a relationship, loose a job. The list is endless.

I say *must* because, even if you believe that you are not so driven—and, of course, you are probably right—the world around you is driven. As part of that world, you automatically and necessarily pick up that driven quality. It's a principle called entrainment: individuals in a system necessarily adopt the rhythms and movements of the systems in which they live.

I experienced this late in life. In my early forties, I was functioning as a true manic within the system. I didn't know what to do, but I knew enough to know that, if I didn't do something quickly, I would be in serious trouble. So I went away alone to the Northern California coast and stayed there for a month. I just "stopped"—cold turkey. It was difficult to arrange. It inconvenienced and annoyed others. But it was life-changing. It was the "something" that I did. No more manic life for me.

What will you do to keep from being swallowed up by the manic culture that we have created for ourselves? Will you survive? Even thrive? Will you be able to give this example to your children or to others you care about? What you do to respond to this mania is not nearly as important as that fact that you *do something*. And don't stop. Just keep doing it.

It's not what you do; it's that you **do something!**

And Keep Doing It

— :: —

One antidote to stress is self-expression. That's what happens to me every day. My thoughts get off my chest, down my sleeves and onto my pad.

—Garson Kanin

Once you've "done something," you must sustain it. To overcome the stress that a manic society places on you and in you, you can't just do something once and be done with it. You've got to keep on doing it.

American writer and film director Garson Kanin tells us what worked for him: writing. By writing, he moved the stress out of himself and onto the page. It was his ongoing way of doing something in response to the manic, driven, and stressful culture in which he lived. Notice he says this is "one antidote" among many and it "happens every day."

Now writing may not work for you. But remember, it's not *what* you do; it's that you do *something!* What is your something?

Music? Walking? Exercise at the gym? Meditation? Gardening? A hobby? Sewing? This is an extremely practical and personal decision without a lot of rules. Simply do what works for you. What takes you out of the moment for a while? What calms your spirit and pleases your body? What quiets your soul and brings you to a time of inner peace?

Some will know immediately what works for them; others will have to consider for a while, perhaps even choose to try something for the first time that will become their "something."

I'm with Garson Kanin. No matter what I'm writing, I'm always taking something from within me and moving it out of me. It's an isolated kind of activity and thus quieting to me. Add walking and hiking and you know my "somethings."

This not merely an option, but an urgent necessity for healthy, wise 21st-century living.

Find your "something" now—or very soon.

Expectations

— :: —

There have been a lot of nuts elected to the United States Senate.

    —Senator Charles Grassley

We are a young country compared to some others—newborn compared to many. Some "newer" countries may have been recently "created," renamed, reorganized, or changed boundaries. As a national culture, however, we're still the new kids on the block—and it shows.

I find one of the ways in which our inexperience shows particularly harmful—that is, the way we treat our public and elected officials. We come down somewhere between being naïve and judgmental. Publicly, we seem to expect nothing less than perfection of them. Any rift in their moral fiber, even any human foible, and we viciously attack them and strip them of their moral authority. Thus, hiding and feinting and deception become a way of life for them.

It's revealing to watch politicians, for example, as they squirm every which way to avoid any hint of weakness or doubt, any lack of knowledge or even any mistake. Or when they lie outright about something they've been caught doing. Of course they have weaknesses and doubts; of course they lack information; and, oh yes, they do some stupid things! Who doesn't? They're human beings. Why don't we allow that? Our unrealistic expectations literally force them, I believe, into dissembling at best, and lying and living double lives at worst. We see examples of politicians and others who are caught in the trap every week in the news.

Of course, there is a thin and difficult-to-define line between being human and making mistakes, and being downright incompetent and deceptive. Of course we should not condone incompetence and deception. But human foibles?

Politicians are so careful, so programmed and scripted, so "created" by image-makers, so spun and made-up, that it's hard to know them as real people. Thus, as Senator Grassley reminds us, we have elected many nuts to Congress.

I think we have to take some responsibility for that. We need to allow our leaders to be as human as we are. Of course we want them to be noble and exemplary individuals; but when they show human foibles and weaknesses, we should recognize ourselves in them and simply accept it as human nature.

Forgive-a-Public-Official Week?

Patriotism

— :: —

You're not to be so blind with patriotism that you can't face reality. Wrong is wrong, no matter who does it or says it.

—Malcolm X

Malcolm X is one of those people about whom you can say almost anything and it could be true. What he says here, however, I certainly believe captures an important truth.

"My country, right or wrong" is an expression that probably originated with a speech given by an enthusiastic naval commander in 1816. In these days of heightened fear of terrorism, however, it is probably not "politically correct" to argue against the dictum. Too bad.

I understand patriotism to be love for and devotion to one's country. But loving a country is like loving anyone or anything—it should not exclude criticism. If it did, it would be dumb and blind. To accuse those who voice their criticism of their country of being unpatriotic is absurd. It's only a short trip down that road to communism, or oligarchy, or theocracy.

I was having a casual conversation with a passing acquaintance, a thirty-something Canadian woman, while on a recent trip to Vancouver. As we waited for an elevator, I mentioned that I had just arrived from California. In response, she said that her brother had invited her to live with him and his family in Arizona. Then she said, "I just don't think I want to live in the U.S. It's so . . . . so . . . I don't know . . . pushy. Everyone's so hyper!"

I responded with something like, "Yes, I know what you mean, especially from a Canadian's point of view. I think our country is going through a hard time right now. I hope . . . ." But before I could finish, she gasped, "You're an American!? I'm so very sorry!" In the circumstances, it was understandable she'd assumed I was a fellow Canadian. Typically Canadian, she felt very bad about what she considered an inappropriate comment about my country. I again assured her that I really understood her comment and was not offended, because I could not disagree with the "pushy" and "hyper" parts. In fact, they seemed quite accurate to me—even understated, compared to what many in the world were thinking at the time.

America, I love you! But . . . !

Cheerful Evil

— :: —

Men never do evil so completely and cheerfully as when they do it from a religious conviction.

—Blaise Pascal

Pascal lived and wrote in the mid 17th century, three and a half centuries before 9-11-01. Evil, especially violence, has *always* been a challenge for religions.

History clearly shows that religious people become so convinced of their beliefs that they deem them worthy of forceful promulgation and defense—even a defense that contradicts some of the very doctrines the religion promotes. Indeed, these defenses have often turned into brutal offence.

Of course, religious beliefs, by their very nature, are empirically non-provable. Thus, the defenses and the differences persist. Who can prove someone wrong when God is the source of that person's knowledge?

Thus the question: What can contemporary believers do about religious violence?

> They can ignore their past, and in some cases their present, behavior and simply carry on, doggedly embracing the faith of their fathers.

> They can become secular humanists, separate religion and spirituality and themselves from the community of believers, and let organized religion go on without them.

> They can remain active, believing members of their religious organizations and work for reform from the inside, calling prophetically for peace and a return to the peaceful core principles of all religions.

> They can accept all religions as true insofar as they embody part of the whole truth about God.

I believe your immediate or specific answer to the question is not as important as your acknowledgment that it is a vitally important and real question that deserves a thoughtful and ongoing response.

Wake up to the possible violence in all religious sentiment. Take some small steps to respond.

True Religion

—::—

It is easy enough to be friendly to one's friends. But to befriend the one who regards himself as your enemy is the quintessence of true religion. The other is mere business.

—Mohandas K. Gandhi

In describing true religion, Gandhi summarily dismisses anything but befriending your enemy as "mere business." It seems very nearly an insult to religionists, however, to call what they do "business," let alone "mere business." To say that Gandhi had strong feelings upon which he staked his life is an understatement. He had feelings about what is called "true religion"—true, not in the sense of "the one and the only," but in the sense of authentic.

Many years ago, I had a theology teacher whose mantra in and out of class was "Be kind!" He repeated it so often that we imitated the way he said it and, in the typical way of students, mocked him for what seemed to us at the time an oversimplification, or at least a mouthing of the self-evident. How wrong we were.

Consider all of the facets of religion, all of the liturgies and services, all the dogmas and teachings, all the practices and moral injunctions, all the beliefs and customs, all the gatherings and identities, all the history and all the writings. They mean little or even nothing if the followers of the faith are not kind to other people, especially to enemies.

Kindness to all is where the religious rubber meets the social road. It's the only true measure of success for a religious practitioner. It is, as Gandhi says, the quintessence of authentic religion. The rest, by comparison, is not much. Our beliefs are important only insofar as they contribute to our day-to-day kindness to others.

By this standard, how successful a religionist are you? What do you make of non-religious people who are truly kind to others? If you're like me, you'll experience some dilemma and unrest as you answer these questions.

Be kind! Especially to your enemies.

The High Road

— :: —

The Holy Prophet Mohammed came into this world and taught us: "That man is a Muslim who never hurts anyone by word or deed, but who works for the benefit and happiness of God's creatures. Belief in God is to love one's fellow men."

—Abdul Ghaffar Khan

What good-intentioned religionist could find fault with that statement? Indeed, one can easily, in the place of "Muslim," substitute "Christian," "Buddhist," "Confucian," "Hindu," "Humanist," and so on.

Our nation is face to face with a golden opportunity to chose the high road as we deal in a very concrete and painful way with the religion of Muslims.

As I see it, the high road consists simply in 1. taking the broad view and 2. knowing history.

1. The broad view: Human beings tend to pre-judge people they do not know, especially when their first encounter with them is not an expression of the entire group but of that group's worst, most violent, and fundamentalist side. If we continue to do what human

beings tend to do, we are taking the low road, not the high road.

2. Knowing history: When the President bumbled into using the word "crusade" as he spoke of his war on terror, he betrayed a dreadful lack of knowledge of history, unfortunately typical of so many of us. The Crusades (1095–1291) of the Middle Ages represents one of the most violent and deadly combative eras in history, probably launched by Christians against the Muslims (although still hotly argued) with immense world-wide consequences felt to the present era. The use of the word was like waving a red flag at a bull.

I hope it is clear that I am saying nothing about the necessity of justice meted to perpetrators, active defense, etc.

We in the West have encountered the Muslim world, many of us for the first time really, by an expression of its fundamentalist extremists. Will we allow that expression to carry the day and to speak for the whole? That would be taking the low road, not the high road.

Waking up so often involves non-conformity, going against the grain, opposing the popular view, no matter your political persuasion.

But it is the High Road. Better view!

Eternity

— :: —

Everybody knows in their bones that something is eternal, and that something has to do with human beings.

—Thornton Wilder

In the last decade, several important and popular books have been published in defense of atheism and the negative aspects of religion and churches in general. Several of these works have had long runs on the best-seller list. I have read a couple and have learned from them.

What's good about these books—at least those I've read—is that they don't pull any punches when it comes to critical analysis of their subjects. Our culture, on the whole, is deferential to religion and hesitates to criticize it publicly. None of that for these authors. No topics are off limits; no automatic niceties are spouted simply because the argument deals with churches.

However, it surprises me that, so often, these writers' works are one-sided. I suppose they don't see their books as debates or as dealing with a multi-faceted issue, but simply as commentaries on a subject from one point of view. I think they throw out the baby with the bathwater.

What they seem to miss is the inevitability of religion and its essential contributions.

Whenever people gather together in the name of the metaphysical, the spiritual, or the divine, that gathering will, given enough time, become what we call a religion. Its beliefs and practices will eventually become systematized and institutionalized. You can call it something else, but what it is is a religion—a system of beliefs and practices held to with faith, an attempt to answer the Big Questions about the meaning of life and the nature of eternity. *Everybody knows in their bones that something is eternal.*

What these writers leave unsaid, or grace with only passing lip service, is that religion has contributed, and continues to contribute, an immense amount of service and care, and provides a structure for spirituality and community for millions of people. *And that something has to do with human beings.*

However, the atheists make an important contribution as well. They keep topics open to discussion and say things that many people have long thought but dared not say. If, indeed, what is eternal has to do with human beings, then the first thing we have to do is tell each other what is in our hearts.

We can begin, you and I, by telling someone.

Cooperation

— :: —

One religion is as true as another.

—Robert Burton

The meaning of the word *ecumenical* is "promoting or encouraging worldwide religious unity or cooperation; churches supporting each other."The insistence of religions on their exclusive embodiment of the truth is a scandal of human religious history—in my humble opinion.

Robert Burton was a 16th-century English scholar and cleric. Do you believe his comment quoted above? I do. And that puts me in perhaps the highest rank of heretics, no matter which religion is making the exclusive claim on truth. Or, more positively stated, it puts me in the ranks of the little-known Perennialists.

Perennialism, sometimes referred to as Traditionalism, was begun by René Guénon (1886–1951) and is encouraged today by a small number of philosophers. I mention it as an example of an attempt to resolve the "one true religion" question. A fascinating combination of typically "liberal" (all religions are indeed part of one great religion) and "conservative" (anything modern or progressive, humanist or egalitarian, is wrong and perverse), Perennialism is an effort to transcend religious exclusivity.

Frithjof Schuon, Perennialism's best known adherent of the past century, said that the idea that a single religion could monopolize God is not only an error, but an absurdity. The answer, he claims, is to select the religion that suits you best and become a devotee. The key is to distinguish religion's external form from its internal dimensions. Pick and choose from the former and embrace the latter as one way, your way, to God.

This is certainly an oversimplification, and there are many challenges to the theory. But the philosophy stands as a system that comes to grips with the question that ecumenists like to avoid—all major religions claim to be the only true religion.

It also presents modern thinkers with important questions to ponder. Can you be both open and accepting of all religions while remaining seriously devoted to your own chosen one? Can you accept that the more devoted you are to the practice of your faith, the more you are testifying to the truth of other faiths?

Burton, Guénon, and Schuon would answer yes to these questions. Perhaps they can serve as models for those of us who also want to acknowledge the major ecumenical challenge for all religions.

> Now is the hour to hear the voice crying out in the wilderness.

CHAPTER 5

Our Differences

— :: —

Tragic Enigma

There is a strange kind of tragic enigma associated with the problem of racism. No one, or almost no one, wishes to see themselves as racist; still racism persists, real and tenacious.

—Albert Memmi

Which of us would acknowledge that he or she is a racist? That we judge someone in a negative way because of skin color or other bodily or cultural characteristics? My guess is that very few of us would make such an admission. Yet, all of us—yes, I believe virtually all of us—are guilty of just that. Memmi, a Tunisian Jewish writer who lives in France, calls it a "tragic enigma."

The term is provocative. The phenomenon of racism, Memmi says, is enigmatic, difficult to understand, or inscrutable, or obscure. Is it? Well, on one level, yes. It's not logical. To be prejudiced against someone simply because they are different does not make any sense. And yet, the reluctance to acknowledge racism in ourselves is not so hard to understand.

"Tragic," I would not argue with. Throughout history, racism has been responsible for the most repugnant, the most vile, the most inhuman crimes against humanity.

You and me and racism? For my part, I acknowledge that I have been, and still am, a racist. It deeply shames me to acknowledge that. I hate racism, especially when I recognize it in myself. But acknowledgement is the very first step in conversion, in growth. I believe this is the underlying implication of Memmi's words. You cannot transform a personal attitude like racism unless you first acknowledge that you personally have it—shame be damned. Then you can start the process of change; but not before. It's only logical.

And you? Please take a moment to look at the real possibility that there is racism in you. It's probably there. Probably not in any overwhelming or horrible way, but there nonetheless. And it's the accumulation of those seemingly minor attitudes in you and me that gives truth to Memmi's description of racism as a "tragic enigma" that persists, real and tenacious."

The truth please: Are you racist? Acknowledgement is the beginning of freedom.

I or We

— :: —

I have been searching for friends for months, ever since I have been in this country, and I still have not been able to find them. Where do young people gather?

—College exchange-student from Europe

This young woman was in a good deal of pain, frustration, and loneliness when she spoke these words far from home. Her custom there was to meet with a large group of friends and acquaintances after and between classes in a café near the university. She and her contemporaries spent many hours together talking, drinking coffee, and generally hanging out and getting to know each other. Then they all headed back to their respective homes. They gathered on weekends too—in a church or a café, or some other public venue.

"Where are these places here?" she wanted to know. "Everyone runs off someplace after classes and I don't know where they go!"

This is just one of many cultural differences between Central Europe and America. We tend toward the individualistic; they tend toward the communal. I felt very bad for this client who came to my counseling practice. She did not really need psychotherapy, just some help adapting to a foreign and seemingly unfriendly culture. How could I answer her question? Where did her school mates gather? I didn't know. I asked some college-age friends and acquaintances. They didn't know. "We really don't hang out much in groups," one said, "but more with one or two other friends, or maybe a group of a few more."

The truth is that we are not a very communal society. Much of our socializing and time spent with friends is with one or just a few others. Often, this happens in our homes and not in a public place. And it is very rare that others feel free to join us, uninvited, in a public place.

Pity. At least I think so.

Ambiguity

— :: —

The awareness of the ambiguity of one's highest achievements (as well as one's deepest failures) is a definite symptom of maturity.

—Paul Tillich

Tillich's compelling statement emanates hope. Awaken to ambiguity, awaken to wisdom. Nothing is so successful that it has no negative results. Neither is any failure so abject that it projects no light at all.

I think this can be true of a nation as well. Today, we seem to be living in a period characterized by a deep disquiet—on both sides of our political and social divides. As a nation, we seem divided into two extreme camps of angry, narrow-minded bigots and wildly liberal, anti-family socialists. Why such extremes? The American political system grew out of compromise. We used to argue about politics with people who disagreed with us. Now we only seem to talk with those hold our views.

Why all this vitriol? It has to come from somewhere! Yes, the buck stops right here. Ultimately, we all have to acknowledge: "It comes from me!"

Tillich's "symptom of maturity" implies that, no matter what state we're in now, it can be better. The key is to find the good in what we see around us and emphasize it. What steps can we take to compromise, to see the other point of view, to appreciate others' needs? There is no opinion from which some good cannot come; there is no opinion that does have a negative side.

No, this isn't "pie-in-the-sky" sweetness and light. It's the way democratic politics must work, because it's the only way it does work. We have to talk to each other and compromise. And, at the end of the day, we have to cook some burgers together and all go home. We can and must at times say, "I disagree with you!"—by all means! What we could say is, "I disagree with you, but I respect you." And what we really should say is, "I disagree with you, but I like you!" Be still my heart!

Are you awakened to ambiguity? Could you give it a try?

Racism (Without Comment)

—— :: ——

Racism is man's greatest threat to man—the maximum of hatred for a minimum of reason.

—Abraham J. Heschel, American rabbi

Lukewarm acceptance is more bewildering than outright rejection.

—Martin Luther King, Jr., civil rights activist

At the heart of racism is the religious assertion that God made a creative mistake when He brought some people into being.

—Friedrich Otto Hertz, Viennese-born sociologist

It demands a great spiritual resilience not to hate the hater whose foot is on your neck, and an even greater miracle of perception and charity not to teach your child to hate.

—James Baldwin, American writer

Accomplishments have no color.

—Leontyne Price, opera singer

I never believed in Santa Claus because I knew that no white man would be coming into my neighborhood after dark.

—Dick Gregory, comedian

I imagine one of the reasons people cling to their hates so stubbornly is because they sense, once hate is gone, they will have to deal with their pain.

—James Baldwin, American writer

We hate some persons because we do not know them; and we will not know them because we hate them.

—Charles Caleb Colton, English cleric

We learn to be racist, therefore we can learn not to be racist. Racism is not genetic. It has everything to do with power.

—Jane Elliot, American teacher and activist

Prejudice is the child of ignorance.

—William Hazlitt, 18th-century English writer

It's never too late to give up our prejudices.

—Henry David Thoreau, American essayist

Try not only to think about these ideas, but to feel them. It's the only way they'll change you.

Awaken to Identity

— :: —

It is a great shock at the age of five or six to find that in a world of Gary Coopers you are the Indian.

—James Baldwin

There is more to this brief quote than may at first be evident. The players are a typical Western movie hero of the 1950s, the Indian whom the Western hero chases and often kills, and James Baldwin, inspired African American novelist, playwright, and poet (1924–1987).

Baldwin certainly speaks from personal experience. Born poor, the first of nine children, he never knew his father. Also born black, gay, and brilliant. What a life he led!

But let's look at his words here. They speak of the shock of first discovering, as a child, that the world is not what it seems, that the world is very dangerous territory, that something is very wrong, and especially that it feels as if there is nothing you can do about it. "Shock" seems too mild a word.

I find some companionship in all three of the characters in this script. As a middle-class white male, I have benefited, like Gary Cooper, from society's granting power to that sub-group. As a gay man and writer, I can, to a small degree, identify with Baldwin and the American Indian, both of whom have been degraded, cheated, and deprived of rights because of who they are.

With whom do you identify here? Are you a Gary Cooper, an Indian, a Baldwin? Maybe more than one?

Try each one on for size, changing gender as necessary. Are you one of the privileged in society? What are the implications of that for you? Or perhaps you are a member of a "minority group" that does not enjoy any automatic privileges, but rather automatically receives negativity and inequality. Or perhaps you can identify with more than one.

Spend a while with some identities that are
different from your own.

Mistaken Identity I

—::—

As far as I'm concerned, being any gender is a drag.

—Patti Smith

Twice in my life, at least that I know of, I have been mistaken for a woman. The first time it happened, I was about seventeen. The mistaken identifier was Paul Brown, world-famous football coach of the Cleveland Browns. To get the full impact of this mistaken identity, please understand that there was probably no one better-known in Cleveland at that time, and probably no one with a more macho reputation.

It was the middle of winter in northern Ohio and bitterly cold. My dad had taken my brother and me skeet shooting. While I was out shooting a round, Paul Brown, a friend of one of the shooters, arrived in the little club house. No one expected him. When I came into the welcome warmth of the tiny space and started taking off all the scarves and hats and ear-muffs I had on, someone introduced me to him. *Wow!* I thought to myself, *Paul Brown!* "Very pleased to meet you Mr. Brown!" I said. To which, with clear disappointment in his voice, he said, "Oh, I thought you were a woman! As I was watching you outside, I was certain you were a woman!" And then he was so surprised by my gender that he said it again—and, I think, even again!

I was immediately self-conscious and embarrassed as well as confused. I think my father was mortified. Brown seemed not to apprehend the discomfort he had caused. Adolescence is fragile enough on its own.

As I look back on that youthful experience from the vantage point of time and history, I can consider it more objectively. Why are males still very uncomfortable if they are mistaken for a woman or considered feminine or womanly? Why is that so bad? The opposite can be true, but probably not as strongly. Trying not to over-interpret, I believe this to be a sign that the patriarchy under which we all operate is as alive and well today as it was in the 1950s. An essential plank in the patriarchal platform is that women are weaker, less capable, and subservient to men. It shows in many ways, large and small—in the glass ceiling that still exists, and in the feelings elicited by a boy's brief encounter with the great, but insensitive, coach.

How would I respond if the same thing happened today? Read on.

Mistaken Identity II

—::—

Professor Bloom is a finished example of the new womanly man.

—James Joyce

My second experience of being mistaken for a woman happened only a couple of years ago. This time, the identifier was a woman and we had never met. She had read my book, *Quiet Mind*, which she liked. In her kind email, she expressed appreciation and also added: "As I read the reflections in your book, I found it very difficult to believe that you are not a woman."

What was I to feel about that? Most men would feel at least uncomfortable with the comment and probably wouldn't tell anyone about it. Indeed, most men reading Joyce's quote above experience a cringing and uncomfortable feeling. Putting "womanly" and "man" together in the same sentence strikes a deep fear. (The man Joyce is talking about is the main character in his novel *Ulysses*.)

So how did I react? After a fleeting—I have to admit—moment of embarrassment and possibly a dash of residual shame, I felt complimented. I wrote back thanking her. I expressed appreciation for her forthright comment and said that I received it as a compliment. So, between my encounter with Paul Brown and this exchange with an appreciative reader, I was able, in some ways, to change my response.

And you? If you are a man and you are reading this book, consider yourself complimented; you probably understand my response. (It's the men who would not read a book like this, even in a plain brown cover, who most likely would not get it.) If you are a woman, you very probably understand intuitively.

However, the trend seems to be changing slowly. Younger men are not as threatened when they are seen as having (typically) feminine traits and interests. That is a much more normal and healthy state of affairs, I believe, simply because it is authentic—it is the outward expression of an inner reality. Even Hollywood is producing examples of straight men portraying women—a practice that is, of course, a very old tradition.

We all are, simply, who we are—with the interests and characteristics that we have. Whether these characteristics are typically masculine or typically feminine is secondary and of little import. It tells us nothing essential about the person.

> *Express your typical other-gender interests and traits! Yes, they are there.*

The Right Thing

— :: —

Black people have never had the power to enforce racism, and so this is something that white America is going to have to work out themselves. If they decide they want to stop it, curtail it, or to do the right thing . . . then it will be done, but not until then.

—Spike Lee

If you asked me to articulate the theme that runs through this book, I would refer you back to the Introduction. I would remind you about terrible innocence and the need to awaken ourselves from pretended sleep. But, I would also answer, "Fear—fear of what is different from us, fear of the unknown, fear of what appears to threaten us, fear of those who disagree with us, fear of what lies outside of our experience. And ultimately, the worst human fear—our fear of each other."

Racism is the embodiment of that fear. Deal with our fears, and we'll deal with our racism—among other things.

Are we really so far from the dark caves of pre-history? From the candle-lit world of the Dark Ages?

Or from the shadowy haunts of medieval times? Sure, the Enlightenment happened. The Renaissance is part of history. The Industrial Revolution made its mark. We live in "modern times." But there still remains that deep spark of fear that will not be extinguished, and that bursts into consuming flame at the slightest provocation. We strike out in anger born of fear.

Wouldn't it be nice if the 21st century became known for conquering, not nations and peoples, but human fears? What an idea!

You and I? If you are part of the "white America" referred to above, then you know in your heart what you can do. If you are not, you also know in your heart that racism is not confined to any one group, and you can look into your heart and know what you must do as well.

Hey, we *all* must "do the right thing." That's the idea! All!

We are all invited to join the human family in doing the right thing.

Tolerance

— :: —

Human diversity makes tolerance more than a virtue; it makes it a requirement for survival.

—Rene Dubos

"Tolerance" is a word I have never liked. Mostly because it seems to indicate that I'll "put up with" someone, but I don't have to like them, or that I'll "endure" your presence, but don't have to enjoy it. Very off-putting, isn't it?

Then I began to think about the word, especially as I came across it in reading. I looked it up: Webster says tolerance is the "capacity to endure pain or hardship: endurance, fortitude, stamina." So far so good. Then comes: "sympathy for beliefs or practices differing from or conflicting with one's own." Still sounds good. Also, "the capacity of the body to endure or become less responsive to a substance (as a drug) or a physiological insult especially with repeated use or exposure." Yes, good.

Then comes the clincher: "the allowable deviation from a standard." And there's the rub! Who gets to determine the "allowable" and the "standard"? Ha! Fine if we're talking about science (the tolerance for error on the machinery is .00002 cm), but not if we're talking about human relations. This use of the word, as in "zero-tolerance," has recently been applied to drug use and criminal behavior, a concept authorities find difficult (impossible?) to enforce.

What Rene Dubos (of "Think globally, act locally" fame) wants to get across is clear: We are all different, but we all gotta get along! He rightly makes tolerance a requirement for human survival.

So the word is not the problem; the problem is what "allowable" means to you and to me. Why is someone's deviance tolerable and someone else's not? Why can we "allow" some differences and "not tolerate" others? Let's keep trying to exchange "tolerance" for "acceptance" and "understanding."

What difference(s) do you not tolerate? Oh.

Queer

—::—

For me to use the word "queer" is a liberation; it was a word that frightened me, but no longer.

—Derek Jarman

I must admit, it also frightened me. I was a long time becoming comfortable with the word "queer." I regret to acknowledge that I still feel edgy about it in certain contexts. The regret comes from a conviction that it is almost certain to become *the* word to indicate anyone who falls into a broad category of sexual minorities—including, but not limited to, lesbians, gay men, bisexuals, and transgenders—anyone who does not fit the "acceptable norm."

To most people born after the late 1970s, it's simply another word meaning something like "not ordinary sexuality." "Queer," however can still be used with vitriol, depending on the mouth from which it emanates.

I certainly have been frustrated with the inexact terms applied to sexual minorities. A current common usage is the awkward LGBTQ, which is inclusive but hardly falls trippingly off the tongue. "Genderqueer" is another variation.

I ask you to examine your comfort level with the word "queer" when it indicates a sexual minority. If you have a degree of discomfort, great or slight, it can be revealing:

> You're of—ahem!—a certain age. Me too. What's the motive behind your reticence? Probably not wanting to offend queer people with the word. After all, it does sound offensive to you. It likely has belonged to the category of "dirty word." No wonder it's hard to use—which is no reason not to use it.

> You're fixated in a former cultural matrix. In other words, the world has gone faster than you have. You're not keeping up. There is a degree of laziness to this that indicates something much broader than the use of a word: resistance to change. Me too.

> You may shock others who hear the word coming from your normally civil and careful lips. They'll be OK. So will you and I.

"We're here. We're queer. Get used to it!" Then let's get on with life.

Times Change

—::—

It is the order of nature and of GOD, that the being of superior faculties and knowledge, and therefore of superior power, should control and dispose of those who are inferior. It is as much in the order of nature, that men should enslave each other, as that other animals should prey upon each other.

—James G. Birney quoting William Harper, 1840

Let woman exert the power which is hers "by endowment of heaven" in the training and strengthening of the moral sentiments, and her vote will be needless, as now it would be ineffectual.

—Rev. Prof. H. M. Goodwin, 1884

The first quote above is from the book *The American Churches, The Bulwarks of American Slavery* by James Birney, a strong anti-slavery voice in the mid 19th century. He is quoting William Harper, lawyer, U.S. senator, chancellor of South Carolina, and circuit court judge. Harper defended the idea that slavery is good for slaves because they will always have work, and that whipping did not harm them, as children are whipped all the time.

He said that without slavery, there can be no accumulation of goods and property, no providence for the future, no taste for comfort or elegancies, which are the essentials of civilized people.

The second quote is from the *New Englander and Yale Review*. Goodwin is a teacher and minister. I quote it here as an example of the way that biblical principles have been applied to the question of women's involvement in politics, specifically voting. It has been only a little more than a century since these biblical principles were understood to be the right ones to apply to this question.

Both men are putting forth their deep and utter convictions of the truth: Slavery is both natural and in keeping with divine will. Allowing women to vote is both against nature and in contradiction with God's will.

Of course, we should not be surprised by these convictions. Anyone who has any knowledge of American history knows them already. But we forget.

Nor has much changed. Can you think of any issues today about which the very same biblical and natural law principles are being hauled out again?

I can.

Diversity (Without Comment)

—::—

I feel my heart break to see a nation ripped apart by its own greatest strength—its diversity.

—Melissa Etheridge, American musician

Uniformity is not nature's way; diversity is nature's way.

—Vandana Shiva, contemporary physicist and activist

No more fatuous chimera has ever infested the brain than that you can control opinions by law or direct belief by statute. . . and the right of debate must be regarded as a sacred right.

—William E. Borah, U.S. senator

There never were in the world two opinions alike, no more than two hairs or two grains; the most universal quality is diversity.

—Michel de Montaigne. 16th-century French essayist

The real death of America will come when everyone is alike.

—James T. Ellison, New York gangster

Peace is not unity in similarity but unity in diversity, in the comparison and conciliation of differences.

—Mikhail Gorbachev, former Soviet president

If we were to wake up some morning and find that everyone was the same race, creed, and color, we would find some other causes for prejudice by noon.

—Howard Aiken, American computer scientist

The diversity of the phenomena of nature is so great, and the treasures hidden in the heavens so rich, precisely in order that the human mind shall never be lacking in fresh nourishment.

—Johannes Kepler, 16th-century astronomer and mathematician

Variety is the spice of life.

—American proverb

If we cannot now end our differences, at least we can help make the world safe for diversity.

—John F. Kennedy, American president

Your quote, your conviction, your thought about diversity?

Reasons and Feelings

— :: —

It is useless to attempt to reason a man out of a thing he was never reasoned into.

—Jonathan Swift

. . . Or a woman, for that matter! (Cut him some slack on the sexist language; Swift wrote in the early 18th century.)

A good forum in which to see the accuracy of Swift's insight is the current intense and public discussion/argumentation/polemic in our country and much of the world about gay people. The principle, however, is valid, no matter the subject. Its implications affect everyone.

Time and time again, I have seen people trying (as I have tried) to change other people's attitudes toward gay people by means of rational arguments based on history, ethics, psychology, sociology, and theology. In the end, however, many people—most often intelligent people—simply do not change their opinions. Arguments do not change them, and Swift tells us why: Because they did not reach their opinion by means of a rational process. By that, I don't mean that they are "irrational." No. Their process of arriving at their convictions simply was not a rational one. It was a-rational, emotional, and most often was probably arrived at through religious teaching.

You have to get out of an idea the same way you got into it, Swift tells us. Thus, the road to change (one could call it conversion) is in the realm of the emotions, of feelings, of community, of love, and of relationships. Because that is where the idea took root.

People begin to change their negative feelings when they have living experiences that tell them something different—when they encounter a person who gives lie to a stereotype; when they get to know their lawyer Susan, a lesbian with whom they have worked for years; when they interact with Jerry the mail carrier, the father of a gay son; when their daughter finally "comes out of the closet" and tells them all of who she is; or when they encounter someone whose experience has moved them beyond the merely rational.

Maybe you . . . ?

Peacemaking

— :: —

Difference is the essence of humanity. Difference is an accident of birth and it should therefore never be the source of hatred or conflict. The answer to difference is to respect it. Therein lies a most fundamental principle of peace: respect for diversity.

—John Hume

John Hume knows from experience. He is the only one to receive the three major peace awards: the Nobel Peace Prize, the Martin Luther King Award, and the Gandhi Peace Prize. He is from Northern Ireland and is one of the major architects of the Northern Ireland peace process.

How desperately we need to learn the lesson he expresses above. The words are taken directly from his acceptance speech to the Nobel committee in Oslo in 1998.

Please go back to those words and read them again.

Note that his subject is peace—not diversity. He gets to differences and diversity through the inherent necessities of peace. He has discovered the heart of peacemaking: respect for the differences among us.

➤ Not fear. Especially not fear!

➤ Not anger.

➤ Not exclusion.

➤ Not avoidance.

➤ Not embarrassment.

➤ Not even doubt or hesitation.

➤ Respect.

That can be an understandably long road for many of us. Our inherited prejudices, our old and deep habits, our lack of exposure to people different from us, our fears—always our fears—keep us stuck.

Please join the diverse throng of humanity in a cry for peace!

Find practical *steps to take. Take them today, this week. Never stop!*

Religious Illiterates

—::—

Americans are both deeply religious and profoundly ignorant about religion.

—Stephen Prothero

Prothero has written a book in which he makes a convincing case, backed up by surveys and research, for the incredible ignorance of most Americans with regard to religion.

It derives, he claims, from an interesting combination of belief without adequate, or sometimes hardly any, knowledge of the system in which you believe—its origins, its development, the reasons for its teachings, or the true meaning of its sacred texts. The result seems to be religions based on emotional conviction, or feeling, or habit, or simply religion by default.

What are some implications of this situation?

➤ Anti-intellectualism, a staple in many religions, seems to be alive and well in North America today. We seem to be saying: *Don't bother me with the details, the challenges; I want to be comfortable.*

➤ Religious illiteracy is the norm. This is harmful because religion is so volatile, so capable historically and actually of rallying the faithful for causes that may not be understood.

➤ Has religion become for us more a matter of habit, of family custom, of inherited tradition, rather than any true conviction?

➤ The types of religion that are especially flourishing in our culture are clearly the ones that emphasize unquestioning commitment.

➤ The intellectual content of these same churches is focused, sometimes exclusively, on the spiritual interpretation of the Bible (or other sacred text), interpretations which can, and often do, differ radically.

Put together your faith and your intellect. Using one without the other leads to perilous naïveté or dangerous aggression. Bringing them together can only lead to integration, both personal and public.

You and religious literacy: Where do you stand? And what does that mean?

Quoting Scripture

—::—

The right of holding slaves is clearly established by the Holy Scriptures, both by precept (law) and example ... Had the holding of slaves been a moral evil, it cannot be supposed that the inspired Apostles ... would have tolerated it for a moment in the Christian Church.

—Rev. Dr. Richard Furman

When I was in theological training years ago, we had a popular saying: "Even the devil can quote scripture for his own purpose." The above quoted words are from an ordained minister of a large religious denomination, written in its name, to the governor of a southern state in the middle of the 19th century. The slavery issue was much debated during that era. It ruptured of course in the 1860s with the Civil War. Furman was pulling out all the stops in the pro-slavery side of the argument. He went on to say, among many other things, "In proving this subject [slavery] justifiable by Scriptural authority, its morality is also proved; for the Divine Law never sanctions immoral actions."

No moral and sane person (politician or not) would make such a statement today, at least not publicly. But you can change the subject from slavery to various other topics and find such statements quite common.

The fact is, the Scriptures (in this case the Bible) do indeed approve slavery, both in the Hebrew Scriptures as well as the New Testament. It would be difficult (impossible?) to deny that, taking the words at face value. The "inspired Apostles" not only tolerated it, in all probability they practiced it.

Another fact is, in many areas of human behavior and morality, we have simply, necessarily, and wisely moved beyond the morality presented in the Scriptures, any Scriptures (that is any sacred writings: the Upanishads, the Quran, the Hebrew Scriptures, the Gospels and Letters of the New Testament, for example).

When will we understand that a slavish adherence to irrelevant moral proscriptions enhances neither the value of the Scriptures nor the healthy living of human life. Indeed, all sacred writings have so much to offer us for the understanding and practical living of our lives, why damage that wisdom?

Now is the hour.

CHAPTER 6

Spirited Living

— ≈ —

A Call to Now

You are in a beautiful city and you are safe.

—Shoeshine lady

I was wandering around the Vancouver airport feeling annoyed. I had just learned that my flight was delayed five hours, maybe more, due to bad weather on the California coast. Uggh! Disrupted plans.

I decided to take advantage of the moment and get my shoes shined. The woman had a smile on her face as she invited me to take a seat, and she spoke with a strong accent; I guessed she was from Africa. She asked me where I was traveling and, when I told her, I added, "but my flight is delayed at least five hours and it will probably be a lot longer than that. It may even be cancelled." I'm sure she noted my frustration.

She was silent for fully two or three minutes as she polished my shoes. Then she looked up at me: "You are in a beautiful city; and you are safe," she said softly and resumed her work.

It took me a few seconds to identify her words as a response to mine. When I did, I too smiled.

Her words transformed my airport-delay experience from one of stress-producing frustration to one of simply living in the moment and accepting whatever happens as—well, whatever happens.

A gift from a woman poor in the world's goods and services, but rich in the inner life. A gift freely and thoughtfully given to a stranger passing through who, by comparison, probably lives in a world of privilege. A generous gift.

I have since wondered what was going on in her mind and heart during the two or three minutes between the end of my remarks and the beginning of hers. What prompted her to respond as she did? I can only conclude that it was simply an expression of the mindfulness that has become a way of life for her, an articulation of who she was.

When I paid her and was leaving, I said, "Thanks very much—and not just for the shoeshine." She smiled.

Live for now—no matter what it is.

The Belayer

—— :: ——

*Learning to belay is one of the most fundamental links
to successful climbing, but true belaying goes beyond
what you learn at the gym.*

—Web page on "How to Climb"

The gym I go to is a climbing gym. There, I am sur-
rounded by many towering walls, to which are attached
scores of oddly shaped footholds. Humans scamper up
and up and up. I do not scamper up the walls—let's
make that clear right now. But watching the climbers
makes my exercise routine pass much more quickly.
Why, I wonder, do people climb walls?

The most interesting part of the climbing to me
is the person who stays on the ground, the "belayer."
Every climber has a belayer—a "safety net," a person
on the ground who feeds the rope to the climber, always keeping hold of it, doling it out as needed. The
climber, in turn, attaches the rope to the wall above and
ahead from time to time. Thus, at any given moment,
the climber is safe from falling—at least from falling
very far.

More than occasionally, a climber does "fall." But the belaying system works and the climber is merely left hanging in space in front of the place where he or she fell off the wall. Sometimes, when a fall is sudden and complete, the belayer is pulled up in the air until a balance with the climber is achieved and they both hang suspended. I guess that the climber and belayer have to weigh about the same, but all of this is my uninitiated take on what I see.

I love the metaphoric role of the belayer. Someone always there (I've never seen anyone climb without one) to "catch" you if you fall. A friend whom you trust completely who looks out for your well-being and success in your endeavor. Invariably, climbers and belayers trade places, the belayer becoming the climber, so there is also lot of mutuality—including the sobering thought that encourages care: I'm up there next. As one climber wisely and metaphorically says: "True belaying goes way beyond the gym."

Are you fortunate enough to have a belayer?
Or to be one?

Inner Life

— :: —

The inner life of a human being is a vast and varied realm.

—Edward Hopper

Here, I want to explore the idea of being specifically aware of your inner life, of consciously considering it. In our rush-about world, the inner life is too often one of the first things to go—make that, *reflection* on the inner life is one of the first things to go. The inner life, of course, is a permanent part of us all.

So just what is the inner life? I believe we all truly know the answer to that question, but at the same time, most of us would have a hard time putting an answer into words. Here's an attempt in a rambling description:

The inner life is the life you live when you are alone and just thinking. All that you fantasize and imagine are part of it. It's what you feel when you see someone you like, or someone you dislike. It's your love, understanding, jealousy and all your intangible values. It's what motivates you to do what you do and be who you are. Your inner life determines your character, your virtues, your vices. It generates your love, your hate, your fun, your fears. It holds your secrets. It is your entire emotional life, all your feelings.

Your inner life is the part you keep hidden; at the same time, it is the part whose results everyone sees. Your inner life determines your response to your "outer life," the part of your life that others can perceive— where you go, what you say, your gestures, your smiles, your scowls. And the most important thing to remember about the inner life: It has the power. It controls every aspect of your outer life.

It's where you make contact with the divine. Other words we use for the inner life are soul, mind, self, and spirit.

Of course, the inner life is way too complex to describe in any complete way. As the artist Hopper says, it is "vast and varied." He also says, "Great art is the outward expression of the inner life of the artist."

Spend some time considering, developing, your inner life.

Great art—in one of its millions of forms—could be the result.

Disagreeing

— :: —

As oft as I have gone among men, so oft have I returned less a man. This is what we often experience when we have been a long time in conversation.

—Thomas à Kempis

I spent some time around people,
but fidelity I neither saw nor smelled in them.
It's better to conceal ourselves . . .

—Rumi

The spiritual teachers—one Christian, one Sufi—seem to be saying the same thing quite clearly: the company of other people is not good for one; stay by yourself.

Really? What do you think about that? What is your opinion about those statements? Maybe read them again and consider . . . .

Personally, I take this particular teaching with at least a grain of salt. More honestly, I don't agree with them, at least not for my life. That may be helpful advice for cloistered monks or nuns, but not for me.

It took me a long time to be able to say that. For most of my life, I would not contradict an authoritative teacher like Thomas à Kempis. Indeed, I can remember, as a student, trying diligently to make sense of and find ways to accommodate his advice, thinking *This must be right. How can I find a way to live it?*

I place a high value on solitude, quiet time, and withdrawal from the marketplace. Indeed, I have written extensively on the topic. But everything in balance. The company of people has most often been a gift of enrichment rather than a diminishment for me.

Do you agree with the spiritual masters? Do you have the resourcefulness to disagree? To use a religious metaphor, when you arrive at final judgment, you will not be asked what Thomas à Kempis believed; nor what values Rumi held. You will be asked what *you* believe. What *your* values are. And no whining, *but Thomas said . . . Rumi said . . .* ! Because the question will always come back: What did *you* say?

> *Are there situations in your life in which you need to disagree with authority?*

Drawing a Line

— :: —

Morality, like art, means drawing a line someplace.

—Oscar Wilde

Scandals have always been a part of the human story. But doesn't it seem as if there are more and more of them all the time? Maybe it's just that they are reported with more fervor. Or maybe people get caught more often. Scandals that are not revealed are, of course, not scandals—just secret crimes that people get away with. It makes you wonder how often that happens.

Highly trusted representatives of church, business, government, and education are regularly revealed to have broken their trust, often in very serious ways. This may mean that they were convinced they could "get away with it." And that means a failure of personal and public morality—acting rightly, following your conscience no matter who finds out.

Somewhere along the way, these people failed to draw the line. My guess is that the failure occurred early in their lives. At some point in their day-to-day living, they crossed the line between right and wrong—a line, as we all know, that is sometimes difficult to identify or to recognize for what it is.

Taking five bucks from your mother's purse when you were a kid, after all, is different from embezzling a million from a bank as an adult. Isn't it?

"Small crimes" like this are also frequently moments of self-deception. For example: *This isn't really stealing; after all, he doesn't need it.* Or: *She's so young she won't even remember this.* Or: *I'm smarter than most people with this degree so it really should be mine.* And: *With all the extra hours I put in, the public owes me at least this much.*

I like it that Oscar Wilde (not a stranger to scandal) couples art and morality in his witticism quoted above. The best art is honest. Just like the best life.

> *What lines are you drawing? Not drawing?*
> *What lines do you need to draw?*

Living with a Mess

—::—

*Why should one imagine that when there is a problem
there is always a solution?*

—Terry Eagleton

Eagleton, a British literary critic, questions a common
assumption here. This seems to me a very American
assumption: If something is out of whack there must be
a way to fix it. If you don't like the way something is,
you can always do something to change it.

It's just very difficult for us to be satisfied with a
mess, to acknowledge it's a mess, and then to find a way
to live with it.

When I was about ten years old, there was a family
that lived down the street from us that was gradually
falling apart. The wife-mother was an emotionally dis-
traught woman who periodically retreated to her room
and didn't emerge for weeks. The husband-father was a
perpetually jolly and generous man who seemed to be
unaffected by anything. All the kids in the neighborhood loved him. He made candy for a living and doled

it out to us in abundance. I remember being amazed that an adult gave us so much candy.

Buddy was their twelve-year-old son. From my current perspective, I suspect he was mildly autistic; at that time, he was just sort of a "different" kid. I liked him; we were playmates.

Then the father committed suicide by jumping out the window of their house. The mother retreated into permanent isolation. Buddy was immediately sent off to "military school." In my young eyes, this was the annihilation of a family. They were here; then they were not. I was deeply saddened and sought solace from my own family. They tried everything to give comfort and understanding, but nothing would console me. It was somehow "wrong" in my eyes that this should happen. It was a terrible mess. "There must be something we can do . . . ."

An early lesson in accepting that there may be no solution other than finding a way, my way, to live with something.

What about the messes in your life?

God (Without Comment)

— :: —

The little boy was drawing when his mother noticed and asked, "What are you drawing, Jimmy?" The boy, without looking up, answered, "A picture of God." "But Jimmy," his mother replied, "Nobody knows what God looks like." "They will once I'm finished," the boy said.

—Steven Harrison, author and spiritual speaker

The feeling remains that God is on the journey, too.

—Saint Teresa of Avila

But I always think that the best way to know God is to love many things.

—Vincent van Gogh, Dutch artist

They say that God is everywhere, and yet we always think of Him as somewhat of a recluse.

—Emily Dickinson, American poet

It is easy to understand God as long as you don't try to explain him.

—Joseph Joubert, French essayist

God is not what you imagine or what you think you understand. If you understand, you have failed.

—Saint Augustine, fourth-century saint

I say to mankind, Be not curious about God. For I, who am curious about each, am not curious about God—I hear and behold God in every object, yet understand God not in the least.

—Walt Whitman, American poet

I was six when I saw that everything was God. . . . My sister . . . was drinking her milk, and all of a sudden I saw that she was God, and the milk was God. I mean, all she was doing was pouring God into God, if you know what I mean.

—J.D. Salinger, American novelist

God is a verb, not a noun proper or improper.

—R. Buckminster Fuller, American essayist

God is the tangential point between zero and infinity.

—Alfred Jarry, French writer

When we know what God is, we shall be gods ourselves.

—George Bernard Shaw, Irish playwright

And for you?

Enlightened

— :: —

To be enlightened is simply to be absolutely, uncondi-tionally intimate with this moment. No more. No less.

—Scott Morrison

The key word here for me is "intimate." That's the kind of relationship you have with this particular moment in time, an intimate relationship. Just as when you are intimate with a person, when you are intimate with a moment, you have many layers of awareness. Some of these may be:

> An awareness of the various climates of the place you're in, the elements of time, the prevailing feelings, what's at stake and for whom.

> You have priorities right—what is more important and what is less so.

> An awareness of the ultimate implications of the mo-ment, of its part in the broader matrix of which it is a component.

> A recognition of all that's gone before that may have brought this moment into being.

➤ A sense of the uniqueness of this moment. It has never been; it will never be again. Thus you know its value.

➤ An appreciation of the particular worldly focus of the moment (are you telling a joke, taking a walk, writing a report?)

➤ And of course, you love this moment deeply.

Why not try to be "absolutely, unconditionally intimate" with this moment, right now, as you read these words? Close the book; let your eyes close, softly . . . .

Of course, enlightenment rarely comes all at once, as it did to the Buddha as he sat under the banyan tree. One step at a time, a moment now and again, a glimpse here and there—these are the prized, star-lit experiences that most of us are fortunate to get.

What does it mean to you to be enlightened?
Write out your reflections.

In Medio Stat Virtus

— :: —

Spirituality, in short, became either rock hard or soggy.

   —Terry Eagleton

"Spirituality" is hard to define in a way that captures a consensus; it means different things to different people. Perhaps more accurately, it refers to many different aspects of a few things.

Eagleton, for example, uses the word broadly to describe spirituality and its tendency to become one of two extremes: a "rock hard," unwavering, no-doubts-accepted fundamentalism, and a "soggy," New Age, feel-good, anything-goes attitude.

I believe, for the most part, he's right on both counts. My question is: Is there a middle ground? A Golden Mean?

In Medio Stat Virtus is a Latin phrase, perhaps first found in Horace (65–27 B.C.E.) and often associated with St. Thomas Aquinas (1225–1274). It translates as "Virtue stands in the middle" and means that wisdom follows the moderate position, not the extremes.

Is there a practical, lived expression of spiritual values—a religious sensibility, if you will—that avoids the two extremes of "rocky" and "soggy," and still retains sufficient value and meaning to make positive endowments to its observers and thus to their society? No doubt many religious believers will answer: "Yes, my religion does that."

For me, however, I'm still looking for that middle way. More accurately, I have decided that looking for a spiritual middle way, for now at least, is my own ongoing spiritual way. I have discovered that, for me, it's the looking that satisfies.

I also believe that we are in a propitious time for speaking prophetically (to use biblical language) to the rocky places and to the soggy places. Too hard! Too soft!

And the middle can be a dangerous place. You can be destroyed or ignored there. I recall one situation in which standing in the middle got me into big trouble. The two sides were in all-out battle and guess who got crunched? Those who follow the wisdom of standing in the middle between extremes are vulnerable. They risk becoming neither, and thus becoming, in a word, wishy-washy. Yuck!

You? Rocky ground? Soggy bog? Middle way?

The World at Your Feet

— :: —

You do not need to leave your room. Remain sitting at your table and listen. Do not even listen, simply wait, be quiet, still and solitary. The world will freely offer itself to you to be unmasked, it has no choice, it will roll in ecstasy at your feet.

—Franz Kafka

When I was a kid, I knew Tom as my brother's friend. Tom was about eighteen, a few years older than I, and very popular, with an out-going and happy personality. One summer afternoon, his life changed forever. He dove into a swimming pool with the aim of diving through a rubber inner-tube floating on the surface. He hit the tube and broke his neck. He remained paralyzed from the neck down for the rest of his life.

But, remarkably, that's not the most significant thing about Tom. Much more significant is his life-long response to his injury. I thought of him when I first read Kafka's words above. Motivated by an unusually mature religious faith, and fortified by a strong will for life, Tom invited the world to "roll in ecstasy" at his unmoving feet.

The world arrived in the form of many people who came from far and wide to talk with him and partake of his generous and joyous spirit. But it also arrived—I can think of no other explanation—in the form of an understanding, a depth of being, and a rich inner life that went way beyond his years and experience. Rather than giving in to self-pity, resentment, or anger, Tom chose to accept what was given him and simply "wait, be quiet, still, and solitary."

This is certainly not to say that there were not many messy, difficult, painful, and failed moments in Tom's life; life would not be human without these. But ultimately, he allowed the world to come to him and—in the holiest, noblest, most elegant sense of that word—reveal itself.

When you cannot "leave your room..." What?

God's Mind I

—— :: ——

*I believe today that I am acting in the sense of the
Almighty Creator. I am fighting for the Lord's work. . . .
I go the way that Providence dictates with the assurance
of a sleepwalker.*

—Adolph Hitler

No one can quote Hitler, of course, without considering the political implications of the words. But I want
this reflection to be as a–political as possible.

Whenever I hear the words "God told me," or "This
is the Lord's work," or "I know God wants me to," or
"God's will is," or "I know the mind of God," I get very
concerned.

It's not that I don't believe that we can, in some way,
through a glass darkly, arrive at a plan of action that may
possibly approach the divine plan—I think. But to *know*
a plan to be divine, to *know* that a course of action or
an opinion is God's, is both dangerous and delusional. If
for no other reason (and there are many more) than that
so many people have "known" and continue to "know"
God's will—and they all disagree.

To understand this danger, you need only read history, as the infamous words above reveal. So many human massacres and disasters were led by leaders who believed they were "divinely appointed and informed," and by people who followed those leaders.

We need to wake up on this issue no matter what our specific political or religious convictions and beliefs are. I believe it is compatible with all religious belief systems to know that we cannot, not one of us, in this dimension of human life, in any absolute way, know the divine will.

In fear and trembling, in doubt and with an open heart, in humility, with all the help we can get, we must pursue the divine mind. And then we must be ready to revise, to admit error, and always be able to begin again.

What is the meaning—if any—of "God's mind" for you?

God's Mind II

— :: —

It belongs to me. God told me if I painted it enough I
could have it.

—Georgia O'Keeffe

As I said in the last reflection, when someone says something like "God told me," I really get very concerned,
unless it's Georgia O'Keeffe, the exceptionally gifted
American painter. I'm not at all concerned about her
use of the words. But of course, there's a difference here. I
guess there's an exception to everything. O'Keefe doesn't
really mean she's got a pipeline to the divine mind, does
she? Then what does she mean?

On several levels, I believe she means exactly what
she says—on a metaphorical level, on a spiritual level,
on a most profound level. I can imagine her, with a
blithe smile and her soft, kind eyes, talking in this way
about a tree or a mountain or a flower. And yes, God
did "reward" her with it, "gave" it to her for spending
so much loving time with it. But God would give the

same flower or tree just as easily to you or me if we made the same effort to love it.

O'Keeffe's is not a possessive owning. It's not an exclusive owning. It invites all to the same ownership. It wields no control.

It's easy to tell the difference between God-told-me statements that are worrisome and God-gave-me statements that are welcoming, isn't it? Even if the difference is challenging to express in words.

Actually, God gave me a tree once, a long time ago. For the same reason that he gave the gift to Georgia. I loved the tree, so he said I could have it. I have not seen that tree for over thirty years and I bet it's had some other "owners" in that time. But maybe not; it is a bit isolated and grows next to many other trees.

I also have a lake and a mountain.

Oh, and a quiet little valley.

What things has God given you? It's important to name the gifts. How terribly sad not to be aware of all the things God has given you.

Name a few. Right now.

Self-Righteousness

—— :: ——

The sick do not ask if the hand that smoothes their pillow is pure, nor the dying care if the lips that touch their brow have known the kiss of sin.

—Oscar Wilde

Maybe that's because, often, the sick and dying know they're sick and dying. None of us beyond childhood have "pure" hands and we all know the "kiss of sin," don't we?

And our lack of purity and kisses of sin stay right with us; they are not simply some evil ways of our past that we no longer carry, that we have finally overcome. No. They never stop, never—despite any religious or metaphysical experiences we may have. That's because we are simply human beings, no more, no less. Both noble and debased. And when we forget these truths, self-righteousness has its day!

I had a bout of it last week. Walking on the street in the city, I was "accosted" (my word at the time) by a "homeless street person" (my immediate label for him). He invaded my space, scared me a bit. Boy, did I have a fit of self-righteousness—all in my head, of course, although I probably gave him a dirty look. He was harmless in the end, and I moved on—self-righteously.

The dictionary says the word means "narrow-mindedly moralistic." Ugh! I really dislike this vice when I see it—especially in myself! Ironically, the blindly self-righteous are the most difficult to change. When we are in that state, we don't see the need. Unconscious and unaware self-righteousness is perhaps the most difficult trance from which to awaken. It seems to have built-in properties that keep us from waking up.

When we are smugly self-righteous, we seem conveniently to forget that we are a part of the community. In a worst-case scenario, we feed off the community and bring it down with harsh, projected judgments aimed at those who particularly threaten or anger us. It happens all the time and will happen again—at times with modest results, at other times with world-wide, colossal harm.

Recognize it and rout it out! Begin with yourself.

Holiness

—— :: ——

Being holy is being who you were meant to be, being
your true self, expressing your humanity in the deepest
sense.

—Robert Ellsberg

The word "holy" (like the word "spirituality") is a tricky
one. It suffers from confused, ancient, and inconsistent
use. I embrace Ellsberg's meaning wholeheartedly.

Following Ellsberg, there are some things that holiness is not:

> Sticking merely to a code of religious obligations and
  duties.

> Surrounding yourself with only the auras and trappings
  of (religious) symbolism and language.

> Making harsh moral judgments on those who disagree
  with your moral code, or who practice another.

> Wanting to enforce your opinion and practice of
  religion/spirituality on everyone.

And there some things that holiness implies:

> Embracing human life in all of its myriad forms and expressions. There are billions and billions of ways to be holy.

> Embracing life in the here-and-now, in your day-to-day existences, not waiting for any afterlife.

> Seeking, until the moment of death, a deeper understanding of your calling, your true vocation, your true self.

> Giving life and emphasis to the most noble and the most kind of your inner resources; challenging and transcending the most base.

Often, what appears to be holy is not, and what does not appear to be holy is.

In the end, of course, we know relatively little about what constitutes true holiness, least of all me. Who am I, who are we, to try to define it? We're poor candidates to be sure, but what's a body to do? We must ask these questions and seek these answers. They are too important to ignore. The fact that we can never achieve the whole truth must not keep us from continuing to try. Failure after failure.

Holy shit! This is harder than I thought!

CHAPTER 7

Health and Well-Being

— :: —

Your Health

God bless the physician who warms the speculum or holds your hand or looks into your eyes. . . . Perhaps one aspect of the healthcare debate is a yen to be treated as a whole person.

—Anna Quindlen

We live in a time in which cultural attitudes toward physicians are changing; have changed, really. My parents' generation bestowed a mantel of respect and honor on medical doctors and took their word as gospel. No more; and that's not bad—even according to many doctors.

Physicians need to be seen as human and as capable of mistakes just like any other human. That is a fact that most of us don't want to acknowledge—especially when we're sick.

When you think of what your physician takes on— your physical health in all its aspects—it can be overwhelming. And keep in mind that we expect physicians to be many things: artist, craftsman, scientist, and psychologist, and probably, at times, even more. Add to this the fact that doctors receive little training in patient communication, or bed-side manners. We've all heard stories. Under the circumstances, the majority do amazingly well.

Thus, if you think your doctor is *totally* in charge of your health, think again. You're wrong. You are the only person in charge of your health—especially when you're sick. If you are a parent, you bear that responsibility for your child. The physician can be, probably should be, your primary consultant, the person on whom you depend for information and treatment. But never hesitate to ask questions and always expect complete and honest answers. And include as many others as you deem necessary in your health care.

I have a personal and deep respect for physicians and for the weighty role they play in society. I have an immense empathy for the challenges they face in today's complex society. The question I have concerns their training: When will medical schools realize the importance of the doctor-patient relationship on the health and well-being of both doctor and patient? And when will they adjust their training accordingly?

Does your doctor look you in the eye?

Good Books

— :: —

This book fills a much-needed gap.

—Moses Hadas

I wish I had been clever enough to think of those words, especially when discussing or reviewing a book I didn't like. There are indeed many books that fill much-needed gaps. Nothing is better than something, at least better than this particular something. (Yes, I am aware this is risky for any writer to say.)

The words also remind me how much my reading habits have changed over the years, especially with regard to what I read and what I don't. Simply stated: There are too many excellent and wonderful books to waste time on the poor ones, the un-true ones, the boring ones, the bad ones. Thus I have resolved to stop reading if I discover a book is not a good one, or at least not a good one for me, now.

This is a change. I would never have done that years ago. I would have considered it a failure of resolve, a quitter's attitude. No more. I now put these books aside easily and take up something else.

This resolve to choose only quality has a broader application in life as well. I think it comes with age. The less time I have left to live, the less tolerant (there's that word again) I am of . . . well, of everything. But especially of a book that does not reach out and grab hold of me.

Some books are so good that I like to read them several times. (Recently, I re-read *At Swim, Two Boys* and *Saturday*.) Some I re-read every few years (*Giants in the Earth*). Some I see at the book store several times before I browse them thoroughly enough to buy them. At times, I'm terribly disappointed; at others, I'm enthralled, as I was recently with *On Chesil Beach* and *In Defense of Food*.

I hope you have the happy gift of spending enjoyable, fulfilling, and enlightening time with books.

This gap fills a much-needed book.

What Old People Know

—— :: ——

The great secret that all old people share is that you really haven't changed in seventy or eighty years. Your body changes, but you don't change at all. And that, of course, causes great confusion.

—Doris Lessing

This seems, on its face, to be the worst of all possible admissions. *I have not changed in all these years!* But it's true; from about the age of ten or twelve through old age, your fundamental character and disposition toward life change very little. That is not to say that you cannot grow in certain ways, or become lax in others. But the fundaments of your personality stay alive and active. And what you want to do seems to change even less.

Consider: Do you know a sour old woman who was not a sour young woman? Or a thoughtful old man who was not the same when young? Indeed, our characteristics, both positive and negative, tend to increase in intensity as we age. Your kindly and loving grandmother, if you're lucky enough to have one, was always like that. Certainly, there must be exceptions—those who slowly, gradually change with age.

This results, says British writer Lessing, in confusion. And the confusion is external. It's not your own, it's the world's. When I am old, I know I want to continue to do everything I have always done.

I have been trying all of my life, for example, to become a perky, morning person. No. I awake the same groggy, sleepy self that I was at age ten. Since I was a boy, I have admired activists, but, despite several efforts, I have never been able to become one. And on and on.

What were your values, the values of your world, when you were ten years old? Think back to that year. What was going on in your life? In the world? I'll bet that your values, your convictions, and your passions haven't changed all that much.

In case you have not noticed, this has implications for all those who are not old. What you are now is what you'll be then. Old age is a very short time away, no matter how old you are.

Be today what you would be tomorrow.

Transcendentalism

— :: —

Even as empiricism is winning the mind, transcendentalism continues to win the heart.

—E. O. Wilson

Where are the Transcendentalists when you need them? Thinkers like Emerson, Thoreau, and others inspired us with wisdom and encouraged us to be all we can be. My strongest association with them is from high school English, where I first encountered American Transcendentalism. It is a difficult "ism" to define exactly, but I believe it's accurate to call it a philosophy emphasizing the intuitive and spiritual above the empirical and practical. One buff calls those early American thinkers "cheerleaders of the human spirit." That is exactly how I remember feeling at my first reading of them.

Positive and upbeat, they were the products of a changing national identity in the early years of the 19th century. Ultimately, of course, the movement faded as social theories that emphasized empiricism, competition, and capitalism became more popular and ultimately won the North American day.

I believe that reading the Transcendentalists today can serve you well. Yes, some of their rhetoric seems a bit naïve and surely Emerson's prose is somewhat stilted. Thoreau is certainly an idealist, at least in his early writings. And yet . . . .

And yet, we need their enthusiasm, their confidence in human nature, their hope and their up-beat thinking, their trust in spiritual realities, and, ultimately, their deep care for all human beings.

The words of Henry David Thoreau, certainly one of the most prominent Transcendentalists, still ring true to 21st-century readers. His experiment at Walden Pond remains one of the defining moments in the history of our country and of the American spirit, although it has been eclipsed in recent times by the more practical and rational. I invite you to re-awaken to the American Transcendentalists.

Dust off a volume of Emerson or Thoreau and read.

Junk Food

— :: —

Eat food. Not too much. Mostly plants.

—Michael Pollan

My father was ahead of his time on several cultural phenomena. One of them was calling junk food "junk food" long before we all called it that. "Don't eat that junk (I especially liked potato chips and Coke); it's bad for you. A beer is much better for you than that sweet junk."

It took me woefully long to heed his advice. Unfortunately, I still like junk, although I try not to eat it too much. Maybe most of us like it. Sugar, fat, and salt taste good.

Eating, of course, is a very important part of human life. We should spend a good deal of time considering how well or how badly we do it.

Michael Pollan can help. His book, *In Defense of Food: An Eater's Manifesto,* is a great place either to begin or continue your journey toward right eating. Pollan has an easy style that I find really helpful both in understanding food and in eating it. Here are some of his basic themes:

➤ Eat food, real food—not stuff junked-up with chemicals and additives, but food like carrots and beef and milk and bread.

➤ Don't eat too much. Here is the point I need to heed. And who will join me in telling restaurants to stop making their servings bigger and bigger? And at home, when you're full, who will join me as I stop eating more? (How helpful is that!?)

➤ Eat mostly plants. Eat more veggies than anything else—which is not to say eat only veggies. Pollen's advice is balanced and rings true.

Yes, yes, we have all heard this time and time again. And certainly the issue of food and eating is very complex. It is heavy with social baggage and personally challenging. One of Pollan's encouragements may help: Don't eat anything that your great-grandmother would not recognize as food!

> *"High-tech tomatoes. Mysterious milk. Super-squash. Are we supposed to eat this stuff? Or is it going to eat us?" (Annita Manning).*

Addict

— :: —

O tribe, more beautiful than moonlight,
how can you tolerate your muddy existence?
You who have drowned yourself in the tavern,
Wake up. It is day. Why are you asleep?

—Rumi

The word "addict" comes from the past participle (*addictum*) of a Latin verb (*addicere*) that has various meanings, among them: "to assent to," "to promise," "to surrender to." The past participle has the meanings of "bound," and "pledged." So from its origins, the word "addict" has been neither negative or positive; it means giving yourself to something wholeheartedly.

Contemporary use of the word, however, has clearly become negative. For us, addiction means crossing the boundary between really, really liking something and being unable to control your involvement with it. It implies the persistent and compulsive use of a substance or practice harmful to the user.

Addiction is a consummately human foible, especially for those who happen to have certain personality and lifestyle traits—for example, impulsiveness, sensation seeking, non-conformity, difficulty delaying gratification, social alienation, tolerance for deviance, and a sense of heightened stress.

So, to the point! Wake up to the fact that addiction is not necessarily a moral failure. In fact, I believe it rarely is exclusively so. And wake up to and acknowledge any possible addiction in your own life and the lives of those you love.

How easy it is to avoid recognizing addictive behavior, especially in those close to you. An excuse is always available. And who likes to confront? Combine these facts with the clever denial of those who are addicted, and you have a formula for avoidance—and potential disaster.

The most common addiction in our culture is alcohol—probably because it is socially acceptable to drink alcohol. Addiction, however, can involve any substance or any process/activity, including gambling, religion, smoking, over-eating, even TV-watching. Is there anything out of control in your life? In the lives of those you care about? Why tolerate a "muddy existence" for anyone? Honest, often courageous, acknowledgement is always the first step toward health. Help is available, for you or for another.

> Seek it if you need it, O you of the tribe more
> beautiful than moonlight!

Hurry Up!

—::—

One of the great disadvantages of hurry is that it takes such a long time.

—G. K. Chesterton

Another disadvantage of hurry is that it is often confused with its cousin, speed. Hurry carries with it the connotation of an undue haste, a rushing that is habitual, unnecessary, and complicated by other people's lack of cooperation in what you need to do. Speed is simply moving fast, which is sometimes necessary.

But of all the bad things you can say about hurry, Chesterton names the worst: Hurry is a thief. It robs you of time.

I was about thirty-five, sitting in my boss's office dealing with some issue. We settled the question and finished the discussion, and immediately I began to leave. "What's your hurry, Dave. You always seem to be in a rush. Where's the fire?" These words felt to me like a criticism from someone I respected and admired, so I asked my secretary at the time if she thought I was always in a hurry. She looked at me with a blank stare and I easily remember her words: "Are you kidding. You're just a blur."

A blur? Me? Oh.

A friend confirmed these two opinions and I recalled the Spanish proverb: "If three people say you are an ass, put on a bridle." By extension: if three people say you are a blur, put on the brakes.

Easier said than done. In fact, that experience was the beginning of my involvement with what became *Stopping* and *Quiet Mind*. It has been a long and often challenging road. Moving at a certain pace can easily begin to feel like an essential part of who you are.

Yet, like so many challenging insights into human life, this involves a paradox. The more I paced myself in my daily activities, the more the blur became a defined and approachable person—and the more I got accomplished. I "gained" time.

What's your "blur factor"?

Being Naked

— :: —

We are so narrow minded that we show war, murder, rape, etc. on TV, but we do not allow to be shown one of the most wonderful creations, the human body in its natural form.

—Mario Roman

I had this same thought recently while watching television. A nude woman and man (in a foreign movie) were in their bedroom preparing for bed. Their genitals were obliterated with an out-of-focus smudge. Then two intruders entered and graphically and brutally tied them up. They beat them practically to death, robbed them, and left them bloody and dying. All the while, their genitals were kept carefully blocked from sight.

What does that say about us? One thing it says is that something is completely out of balance in our collective attitudes toward the human body and violence.

'y, it's both crazy and dangerous. Violence is fine; not.

hts about being nude, or seeing people nude:

of our extreme discomfort with the naked 's, I believe, the shame so many of us have about our own bodies. The shame is based on unde-served moral guilt and cultural pressure to have a flawless body. Nobody has a perfect body! Go to any nude beach and you will disabuse yourself of that one.

➤ Another root of the problem is the assumption that, if you are nude, you will be inappropriately sexually active. Why assume that? Is it true for you? Me neither. Crazy thinking. Let's all stop thinking that way, OK?

➤ Psychologists tell us that children who are never allowed to see their parents or siblings naked see nudity as something shocking. That includes many of us. No wonder! Parents, wake up.

Genesis tells us that Adam and Eve "were nude but they were not ashamed." Because God created it, Pope John Paul II claimed, "The human body can remain nude and uncovered and preserve its splendor and its beauty." Even the pope says so. Much of our hesitation to be naked in the presence of others is social custom, lack of exposure (so to speak), and just plain embarrass-ment. But that doesn't have to stop you, right?

> *"What a singular fact for an angel visitant to this earth to carry back in his note-book, that men were forbidden to expose their bodies under the severest penalties!" (Henry David Thoreau).*

Stress

— :: —

Stress is nothing more than a socially acceptable form of mental illness.

—Richard Carlson

Richard Carlson wrote the self-help blockbuster *Don't Sweat the Small Stuff.* He was also kind enough to write an introduction to my book *Stopping.* We lost him far too early in his life to a sudden heart attack about two years ago.

Carlson was a keen observer of the human condition, as well as one of its most insightful and affirming commentators. He calls stress—that everyday, no-one-can-avoid-it, necessary annoyance—a mental illness. Before I had the benefit of his insight, I had not thought stress in that way, although I had given many work- and presentations on the subject.

hat is Carlson on to here? Stress as mental ill-'s is a great example of how the way you deal s depends on how you think about them. If out stress as a necessary, unavoidable evil, you will respond to it one way. If you think about it as a mental illness that can be treated and overcome or successfully managed, you will respond in quite a different way.

We Americans seem to "wear" our stress like a badge of achievement—as a sign that we are on the leading edge, in the ranks of the work-obsessed and successful. Baloney! Another sign of institutionalized craziness.

Stress is a mental illness that occurs when the person-environment relationship leads us to perceive a discrepancy between the demands of life and our own resources to respond successfully.

As in any mental illness, there are methods either to correct this perceived imbalance or to adapt to and cope with it successfully. There are tons of books and Web sites ready to help you and give you tools. What are you waiting for?

How do you think about stress?

Closets

—— :: ——

One [person's] transparency is another's humiliation.

    —Gerry Adams

Northern Irishman Gerry Adams, president of Sinn Féin, knows what he's talking about here. Life and death.

One of the consequential metaphors of the 20th century is "coming out of the closet." It is significant because it strikes a universal chord in the human heart. It was, and still is, used to describe the process of public self-acknowledgement of gay people. It has become, however, a metaphor to describe the process of integration between our internal self-knowledge and what we are willing to tell the world. It's about integration. It's about transparency. It's also about accepting or not accepting the *belief* that to be known for who you are will bring you trouble.

Living in the closet can imply secrets, double lives, and possibly shame. And it always means fear. I swung my closet door open about thirty years ago and welcomed transparency with gratitude and relief. What I found, of course, were more closet doors behind the one I opened, ones I had not even realized were there. Oh, no! Thus my process continues.

And you? From what closet do you need to free yourself? Anything can form the walls. I've known closet drinkers, closet drug-users, and closet gamblers. But I've also known closet belly-dancers, closet nudists, closet religious adherents, closet atheists, and closet artists. And closet joggers, closet letter-writers, closet knitters, closet whatever-you-keep-secret-from-the-world. Whatever obscures your transparency, whatever you believe will hurt you in some way if revealed, can become your closet.

This is not to say that it is not ever a good practice to keep some things to yourself. When giving donations, for example, you may choose not to "let your left hand know what your right hand is doing," but that's not generally your challenge. The real challenge always has to do with fear—real or perceived.

Come out! Come out! Wherever you are!

Morning

— :: —

The average, healthy, well-adjusted adult gets up at seven-thirty in the morning feeling just plain terrible.

—Jean Kerr

In the interest of practicing the transparency and awareness that I preach, I must make, well, not a confession exactly, but an admission.

I greet (using that word very loosely) every morning in a total fog of groggy semi-awareness barely different from the nether world of sleep and dreams whence I've partially emerged. Happily, this lasts only a half-hour, but, during that time, I'm totally worthless, incoherent, and unaware. It is a particularly vexing characteristic, one that I have been trying to change literally all my life.

More recently, I have let up on myself a bit and allowed my foggy morning state simply to be a part of who I am. If I have not changed it by now, well . . . .

The real problem with this somnambulant state is that it fosters sleeping late, because the later I get up, the less foggy I am. But sleeping in is a trait that is not only un-American; it is suspect from the point of view of any self-respecting member of the high-achieving, consumer culture of the West. So I feel guilty. I hear, "You're just getting up!? I've got half a day's work in!" or "I've already been jogging, had a healthy breakfast, and answered my e-mail."

Adding to my frustration is the fact that I truly love to *be* up and awake in the very early morning, to greet the dawn. It is a time of day I love and appreciate—and rarely see.

So here I make a plea to you rise-and-shiners for those of us who are constitutionally pre-destined (is that stretching it too far?) to awake in a deep morning fog and, thus, to be late risers, sleepers-in. Be aware of our less-than-perfect state. Be understanding of it. In fact, don't notice it and *never* comment on it.

> *If we were meant to pop out of bed in the morning,*
> *we would all sleep in toasters.*

Fun

—— :: ——

If you obey all the rules, you miss all the fun.

    —Katharine Hepburn

The trick, of course, is to know which rules you can break and when to break them. But break them we must if we are to have any fun.

There was a time in my life, quite a long period of time, actually, when I was—how shall I say it?—not exactly a bag of laughs. Kept all the rules—and there were a lot of them. Severe and serious were the virtues of the day and I had a strict limit on fun. So I, in turn, was not much fun to be around. My loss, my regret.

But that was years ago, and now I have a lot more fun. I break a lot more rules. I count myself one of the fortunate ones.

Too many of us are hobbled in our desire to have fun by the expectations of the contemporary world and our perceptions of how we need to behave in it. Thus we lead lives that are not much fun.

Look at this the way Kate Hepburn did. Look for the rules you can break. Which ones can you get away with breaking? Which ones can you break without paying too high a price if you are caught?

The rules I'm talking about are generally considered "unwritten rules," but they can be among the strongest.

Wear something you like that you know will horrify your contemporaries. Say something outlandish that you believe, but never said before. Go somewhere you want to go that you know your friends won't understand. Make friends with someone you like who is an outsider. Sing out loud, whether or not you have good voice.

Clearly, there are a lot of unwritten rules—societal expectations, really—that you can break and have fun breaking. And then there are the "written rules," the more clearly formulated and serious ones. But of course, I couldn't encourage you to have fun breaking those, could I?

"Fun is good" (Dr. Seuss).

CHAPTER 8

Denial and Its Good Friend Death

— :: —

Denial I

It's not denial. I'm just selective about the reality I accept.

—Bill Watterson

Watterson is the creator of the comic strip *Calvin and Hobbes.* As you may know, Calvin is very capable of denial. I can easily picture him saying this to his imaginary/real tiger-companion, Hobbes.

Denial, simply defined, is unconsciously refusing to see unpleasant aspects of reality and replacing them with pleasant, but inaccurate, ones.

But who am I to talk when it comes to being selective about reality? It's so easy. It's so human. These are real quotes from me:

➤ "It's not really raining; the sun will break through any minute." (Reality: Storm immediately follows.)

➤ "No, we just can't afford it!" (Reality: We can; I don't want it.)

> "But we really can afford it!" (Reality: We can't; I want it.)

> "I can be there and back in fifteen minutes, trust me." (Reality: Twenty-five minutes.)

> "I'll just sort of cover this over and no one will notice the difference." (Reality: Everyone saw the difference immediately.)

> "This is a sure bet; it can't go wrong." (Reality: It was obvious to everyone that it would certainly go wrong. It did.)

These are examples of mild and everyday denials. But some denial is more serious—denial of illness, of addiction, of impending financial failure, and ultimately, of death.

Fear, of course, is the main motive for denial. We are afraid of facing reality, often with reason.

So, rather than thinking of *acceptance* as the opposite of denial, perhaps we need to think of *courage*—courage to face the fears, courage to risk failure, courage to be wrong, courage to be embarrassed or to be left holding the bag.

What do you need to face—with courage? Just how will you do that?

Denial II

— :: —

Without a huge admixture of fantasy, reality would grind to a halt.

—Terry Eagleton

Just having railed against denial, here I will defend it, but with a condition: with this type of denial you are, on some level of consciousness, aware of what's going on.

Let's call it creative denial. As writer Terry Eagleton well knows, denial of this sort brings hope.

They were a very likable and popular family: parents, three kids, a live-in grandmother, a foreign-exchange student from Greece, an ever-growing assortment of pets, and lots of aunts, uncles, and cousins in the area, all going about their busy and happy lives with energy and good will. Then the youngest child, 10-year-old Miles, was diagnosed with very serious cancer.

You can imagine how this devastated the entire extended family.

The part of this family's story that I am telling—a story filled with so many acts of love and courage—is a small part about denial, courage, and hope.

While visiting Miles one Saturday morning, I asked, "How ya doin, Miles, my boy?" "Oh, didn't Mom tell you? Today I'm fine, I'm great. Today, all day, I'm not sick at all! We're going to the park and maybe I'll even get to swim. We're all going!"

How easy it was to join into that program! To eagerly jump on that bandwagon of creative denial!

Did Miles or any of his family really think that he was not seriously sick? No, certainly not. But it was a way to allow fantasy to take over and hope to live and have its moment and do its work, to forget the burdens and sadness that illness brings, and simply to have fun when there was not a lot of opportunity to.

That's my kind of denial.

To what situation can you bring the hope of creative denial?

My Monster, Your Monster

— :: —

There's something bloody horrible inside us; a monster. We don't like it so we make out it's not in us personally, we make out it's upstairs or outside or living in someone else's house, and once we've got rid of it, we'll be straight.

—Louise Dean

It's what we don't want to look at, don't want to confront. We do everything we can to ignore and avoid it, pretend it's not there. But it is there. Always will be. Karl Jung gave it a name: the Shadow. It is everything in us that is repressed, unconscious, under-developed, denied, and avoided.

The part that Irish novelist Louise Dean names is the negative part, but the Shadow is not all bad; it contains all the repressed and avoided good parts of us as well. The question is whether we will deal with it wisely—confront it and integrate it—or continue to avoid it and allow it to have its way with us.

We find a clear example of the consequences of not dealing with the Shadow in the politicians, televangelists, and other public officials who destroy themselves with sex scandals, laundering or stealing money, and other dirty deeds that are totally contrary to the public face they present. Representatives of religion and government are stereotypically do-gooders—smiling, happy-faced, wouldn't-harm-a-flea, good-ol'-boy, down-home folks who begin to believe their projected public face. Some of them—the ones who fall—never face their Shadow and it finally has its way with them.

Inevitably, we respond to these scandals by asking how anyone could be dumb enough to risk that kind of behavior, let alone sink so low morally. But they're not dumb. The Shadow will out. When they are caught, their often-silly defenses indicate that they themselves were unaware of the dirty deeds hiding in their Shadow.

The Shadow is happy and helpful when it is known and integrated. The Shadow is unhappy and dangerous when it is avoided and denied.

Yet, along with the monsters within each of us, there are some angels of surprise, generosity, and hidden talents.

The goal isn't "to get rid" of the Shadow and thus get "straight," as Dean rightly implies. Paradoxically, it's by embracing the Shadow—by unpacking and acknowledging it—that we bring integration and spiritual and emotional health to our lives.

>   *Take a step today to name and embrace your*
>   *Shadow.*

Suffering

— :: —

*You know quite well, deep within you, that there is only
a single magic, a single power, a single salvation . . . and
that is called loving. Well, then, love your suffering. Do
not resist it, do not flee from it. It is your aversion that
hurts, nothing else.*

—Herman Hesse

Most adult human beings know in their hearts that
there is no real growth without suffering. At the same
time, most of us know that, more than anything, we
want to avoid suffering. It's only human.

I tried for more than forty years to avoid what
seemed to me the bitterest suffering I could undergo.
I told myself many things: *I can just "avoid" this problem;
I can "cover" it over so no one will see it, including me; I'll
"ignore" it so it will simply disappear; I will carry on as if it
did not exist.*

Finally, forces converged and I gave in. I did not
know it at the time, but I was beginning to follow
Hesse's advice. I was beginning to love my suffering. At
the time, it felt something like suicide.

The particular suffering I had to face is of little importance (that I was gay and always had been). Everyone has different sufferings at different times and in different degrees. Suffering has many names.

I had no idea how I was exhausting myself by not facing my pain—I really thought I was trying to keep suffering at bay, to avoid the pain I knew would simply take over my life. I thought I was avoiding the pain; but I was only increasing it.

And your suffering? Are the sources of your suffering clear? Or do you have to think a moment to identify them? Are they large or small? Some of each? Makes no difference. Are you exhausted by them? Well, then, do as Hesse says: "Love your suffering. Do not resist it, do not flee from it. It is your aversion that hurts, nothing else."

The journey from avoiding your suffering to loving it can bring challenges and disruptions. In my case, there were some messy and painful situations, but no permanent damage. And a whole new life.

Maybe some suffering is just too great to face. I can think of some that I'm not sure I could bring myself to love. But if you can manage it, bringing love to suffering will make a huge difference—not by changing the suffering, but by changing you.

"Well, then . . . ?"

Change in the Air

—::—

As nightfall does not come at once, neither does oppression. In both instances, there's a twilight where everything remains seemingly unchanged, and it is in such twilight that we must be aware of change in the air, however slight, lest we become unwitting victims of the darkness.

—Justice William O. Douglas

It's twilight; have you noticed? Do you notice anything in the air? Something slightly different and new and off-key?

Is there anything that the institutions of the country are doing and becoming that makes you uncomfortable? Makes you squirm a bit? Do you often have, as I do, a desire to withdraw from the ups and downs and craziness of politics and public life and retreat into your own world?

Do you often find yourself angry at the policies and politics of the country? Does this ever lead you to espouse the extreme positions that now are rampant in our nation? The "right" or the "left?" Do you place yourself squarely in one of those groups and reject the other, even express opinions that could be interpreted as hateful of the other? It's the same story for both angry "sides." Oppression is oppression whoever wields it.

Are you aware that many cultures have fallen because they remained unaware of "something in the air" and blithely followed where they were led? Do you realize that a "far-right-winger," a "leftist radical," and all the rest of us in between could answer the above questions in exactly the same way, imagining very different "realities" and threats as they did so?

If we allow ourselves to become "unwitting victims of the darkness" we will all be victims—left, right, and center.

> *Wake up. Watch for signs of "change in the air," your "air."*

Memento Mori

— ∷ —

*I'm going to keep death right here, so that anytime I
even think about getting angry at you or anybody else,
I'll see death and I'll remember.*

— D. Frolov and A. Schneider

What is it that these authors will remember? I think the
answer is "priorities." They'll remember what's important and what isn't, and live their lives as they want to
live them, choose to live them.

I'm also willing to bet that, if you're like me, you've
had a similar thought—maybe just after losing someone
you love—and that, sooner or later, depending on the
impact of the loss, you've gone and forgotten it again.

The old wisdom advises us to keep a symbol of
death close by as a constant visual reminder. *Memento
mori*; remember death. Some monks, for instance, keep
a skull on their desk or sleep in a coffin.

How does all this strike you? If you're like most
in our Western culture, you're squirming a bit because
death makes you somewhat uncomfortable. *Why would
I dwell on death?* you may say. *It's depressing and morbid.*

Think rather of life and all its possibilities and beauty. Death will come soon enough.

Well, yes, of course, but . . . .

Face it, there's nothing like the finality of death to help you keep your priorities in order. Nothing! When you confront your own end, when you know it's over, no more to build on there, finished, final act.

It's not morbid, in the sense of unwholesome, gloomy, or gruesome, to think of these things. It's simply real. You will die. The more you avoid the thought and allow that reality to become fearsome—the more you "don't think about it"—the more likely you are to forget your priorities for living.

Why not try sleeping in your coffin?

Just kidding!

> *But seriously . . . can you say and mean, "I'm going to keep death right here"?*

Nonsense!

— :: —

I like nonsense; it wakes up the brain cells.

—Dr. Seuss

I get an immediate image in my mind's eye when I hear the word "nonsense!" I see actress Maggie Smith in the role of the overly protective spinster/chaperone, Aunt Charlotte, in the film *Room with a View.*" She says that word constantly, in her own convincing way, to her young charge, an unruly and lively niece.

Of course, what she labels "nonsense" almost always turns out to be what inevitably happens, and to good effect for all.

Many of us have an "Aunt Charlotte," and certainly many of us have grown up in a culture that quite successfully mimics her attitude toward anything frivolous and lighthearted. Well, sometimes I suppose we need someone to say "nonsense!" to our proposals. But sometimes we don't. Thank you, Dr. Seuss.

Much of what we eventually accept begins its life in our minds as nonsense:

➤ "Dad, I want to go to art school, not college."
"Nonsense! All my children will go to college."

➤ "I'm concerned about our low sales figures this month." "Nonsense! Simply a summer dip."

➤ "What would you say if I told you I'm quitting my job and moving to Tahiti?" "Nonsense! That's a crazy idea."

➤ "Our country is making a terrible mistake in initiating this war; it will last for years." "Nonsense! We'll be in and out of there in a couple months."

➤ "This home mortgage we're getting seems too good to be true." "Nonsense! Believe me, you'll never regret it."

➤ "I would really love to write fiction!" "Nonsense! You don't have the imagination."

Sometimes nonsense makes sense.

Where You Wind Up

— :: —

If you don't know where you are going, you will wind up somewhere else.

—Yogi Berra

I think a corollary to this wonderfully enigmatic quote from Yogi Berra (aren't all his quotes enigmatic? Do they have to have a point?) is that you *will* end up *some-where.* In other words, you will *not* end up *nowhere.*

Here's what I mean, in the context of Yogi's analogy of a journey. As you travel through life, as you age, you continue to "create" your name, your reputation, how you see and understand yourself, and how the world sees and understands you. You actually create and de-fine reputations for many of your human characteristics. For example, you create your morality, your intellectual abilities, your reputation for kindness, for meanness, for empathy or anger, how you are understood as a worker, as a traveling companion, as a neighbor, and so on.

As you approach the end of your life—or anywhere along the journey—you are never "nowhere," you're always "somewhere." And—here's the point—if you don't know where you are going, as Yogi says, you'll end up where you don't want to be.

You must be awake to the details of the journey. What are your goals? What do you want to accomplish? What is significant to you? What isn't? What parts do you especially enjoy? With whom do you want to travel? What values do you choose for your journey? And so on.

It is truly sad to see a person facing death and regretting his or her life. "Why didn't I do things differently?" "Why didn't somebody tell me?" "How could I have been so blind?" Nope. No good. Too late.

To avoid that, listen to Yogi and spend some time with the big questions. And, if necessary, make some mid-course adjustments.

> *It's actually never too late for anything, is it?*
> *For what is it not too late for you?*

Spending Your Days

— :: —

*How we spend our days is, of course, how we spend
our lives.*

—Annie Dillard

Of course, most of us really don't know when death
will come, but, using the best of "odds and estimations,"
I am well into the last quarter of my life. This perspective has its advantages.

One of them is that I now spend my days a bit
more carefully. I appreciate Annie Dillard's use of the
word "spend." The word implies that I have, like dollars,
just so many years to spend. So, just as with any other
resource, how I spend them is more and more important as the stockpile dwindles.

Some people I have known chose to fill their final
years with as many experiences as they could. From
travels around the world to never-ending projects. For
some, this feels like a pushing against death; for others,
it is just doing what comes naturally.

The challenge for the younger among us, those in
the middle part of life especially, is to realize in some

clear way that the last quarter is totally unpredictable. Some of us don't even get the "last quarter"—or rather, we live it without recognizing it for what it is. Some spend it in debilitated physical health, others in the haze of Alzheimer's or advancing senility. Are these scenarios, or something like them, just around the corner for me? In the road ahead for you?

All of which brings us back to how we "spend our days." What a valuable currency, days!

My today, for example: Up at 7:30; leisurely breakfast with the paper; check my e-mail and then see if I have any desk-work like bills to pay or calls to make. To my studio by mid-morning; write for a couple of hours; lunch alone at my desk. Mid-afternoon exercise for a half-hour, back for some more writing. Home by 5:00 or so to fix dinner for my partner and me. After dinner, maybe some reading, a film or TV; in bed by 11:00 or so.

This is a pretty typical and a very ordinary kind of day. The *only* thing to note about my day is that it's mine. I am spending it.

You and your day? Review how you spent your day.

Late

— :: —

How did it get so late so soon?
Its night before its afternoon.
December is here before its June.
My goodness how the time has flewn.
How did it get so late so soon?

—Dr. Seuss

I have always been late in doing and achieving almost everything in life. At least it seems that way to me. I don't necessarily mean late for appointments or meetings; I do that OK, for the most part. I mean the bigger things, like the stages of development, the steps to maturity.

I have this feeling—intellectually, I know it's crazy, but that doesn't stop me from believing it—that if only I had started everything sooner in life, I could have accomplished so much more.

Time to wake up, I tell myself. The course of your life, especially when you gaze on it from your latter years, can be seen simply as that: the course of your life. Nothing is late, nothing early; it all proceeds as it must—the way it has, the way it will.

Fine, fine, I answer myself. Then why do I still have this feeling that I started everything too late! Answer me that!

➤ Maybe it's because I have to find an excuse for all the things I have not done, that I think I should have done.

➤ Maybe it's because human life is evolving in such a way that there is always more . . . and more . . . and more— but the amount of time remains the same.

➤ Maybe it's because, by this conviction, I will convince the world that there is an immeasurable amount of talent and wisdom that—Good Grief!—will be eternally lost to the ages.

➤ Maybe it's because I fear death and this is as good a way as any to mask that fear.

(I think he thinks too much!)

Near Death

— :: —

One of the near-death-experience truths is that each person integrates their near-death experience into their own pre-existing belief system.

—Jody Long

When snatched from the jaws of death, tooth marks are to be expected.

—Hal Story

I was about ten years old and anxious to show the world that I could do things on my own. One Saturday evening, my aging grandfather, who lived right across the street from us, realized he had run out of cigars. I was dispatched on my bike, with many cautions for care and expedience from my mother, to travel the three-quarters of a mile to buy cigars. (In 1947, they believed you when you said, "They're for my Grandad.")

There was only one heavily trafficked street I had to cross on my way. I negotiated it with no problem on my way to the store. Coming back, however, I almost got killed.

I don't think this really qualifies as a "near-death" experience. That, I believe is reserved for those who literally come "that close" to having their hearts stop— or sometimes even cross that boundary. But from that summer evening to this very day, the experience lives quite strongly in my mind.

As I began to cross the busy street, walking my bike out from between two parked cars, I was sure the way was clear and made a dash for it. The way was not clear and the screech of brakes woke up the entire neighborhood. The car grazed the front tire of my bike. When the car came to a stop, I was looking directly at the driver through his open side window. He was glaring at me, hands tightly gripping the wheel. I looked away quickly, said "thank you" (which I'm sure he didn't hear), and ran the rest of the way across the street through all the stopped traffic.

In some way, my young life had changed. I never told anyone what happened (even though my mother asked about the screeching brakes). But I still feel the "tooth marks."

Bring to mind the occasions in your life when you came closest to death.

How have you "integrated" them? Any tooth marks?

One of These Days

— :: —

Cherry trees will blossom every year;
But I'll disappear for good.
One of these days.

—Philip Whelan

Death, of course stands firmly at the end of everyone's story. *He died of heart failure in January of this year, leaving behind . . . . She died of unknown causes as she was putting the finishing touches on . . . . The couple, married for fifty-three years, died instantly as their car careened off the icy highway and into . . . .*

You and I will have sentences like those written or spoken about us. Only the details will be different.

Have you ever wondered which "one of these days" will be your death-day? Which end date will be carved on your stone? Of course, it will make no difference to you or me; we'll be "disappeared for good." No longer here and part of all this.

Morbid? Useless ramblings?

I sometimes claim, when I am feeling some bravado or perhaps have had a glass of wine or two, that I am not really afraid to die, only afraid of a long terminal illness. The second part of that is certainly true. The first part. . .? I really don't know how true that is or even can be. How can you know for sure if you are afraid of death unless you are indeed dying? Then you will know. No? I think maybe some people may know. But I know I don't.

Whelan, a Zen priest, brings out one fact clearly in his poem. Many of the things around me will live on well beyond my time. The cherry trees will blossom and the Earth will continue spinning. Everything will carry on fine without me. Others will sit in what used to be my chair and live in what used to be my house. Now it will be their chair and their house.

Human life seems long only at its beginning, secure only for the young.

So? Now!

It's all we've got. And it's a treasure!

CHAPTER 9

Knowing Thyself

— :: —

Know Thyself

What is necessary to change a person is to change his awareness of himself.

—Abraham Maslow

When I was a boy, my mother was fond of quoting a particular line from Shakespeare's *Hamlet:*

> This above all: to thine own self be true,
> And it must follow, as the night the day,
> Thou canst not be false to any man (II.78-80).

In the play, the words are spoken by Polonius to Laertes as advice for his son upon going out into the world.

Maslow's insight, I believe, fits well with the Bard's. To be true to yourself, you must first know yourself. And to know yourself, you must have a keen self-awareness. Ah, there's the rub!

Maslow, one of the founders of humanistic psychology, was very interested in "self-actualization" and "peak experiences," and those aspects of human beings that have to do with higher self-awareness.

What about you? Are you self-actualized? That is, do you have the desire to operate, or do you actually operate, at the top of your potential and possibilities? Can you identify some peak experiences in your life? That is, a sudden sense of intense happiness and personal wellness, or even an awareness of "ultimate truth" and the oneness of all things, accompanied by other feelings of well-being?

These are not common questions and concerns for most of us. We're too busy coping with demands and balancing schedules and trying to get everything done that we need to get done.

Once in a while, however, I believe it is important to spend some time with these bigger questions of self-awareness and self-knowledge. In the long run, the time will pay dividends. This is bottom-line wake-up time.

Did I always follow my mother's Shakespearian advice? Sadly no, not always. But I wish I had—and will not cease in the attempt.

Spend some time with: "To thine own self be true."

Giving Power Away

—::—

*If you get the feeling that your doctor doesn't like you,
find another one.*

—Michael Crichton

You may be surprised how many people stay with a physician who clearly indicates a dislike for them. It's the same kind of energy that keeps people giving power in all kinds of abusive relationships: doctor–patient, therapist–patient, lawyer–client, spouse–spouse, barber–customer. Barber?

A memory from young adulthood always comes back to me as I consider this issue—a relationship, if you can call it that, that I had with a barber. Clearly not as significant as a relationship with a physician, but it's the same energy. And the "trauma" of that experience has stayed with me all these years, even though it was a relatively minor incident.

I was seventeen, visiting in a strange city, and needing a haircut. I stopped at a barber shop. I sat and waited my turn. As I looked over the five or six barbers in the shop, I thought *I hope I don't get that one.* In about a minute, *that one* called "next" and I was in the chair. He asked, "How do you like it cut?" When I answered him, he became loudly abusive, saying things like "Who's the barber here?" and "I know what I'm doing so just sit still and be quiet" "You young people think you know everything." These comments were shrill enough for others to hear easily. Now, seventeen-year-olds can certainly be full of themselves, but I did not deserve that kind of treatment.

My first thought, typical of people in abusive relationships, was to ask what I'd done to provoke this. It must be my fault. But I couldn't think where I'd gone wrong. I remember feeling hot and sweaty from embarrassment and sinking into the chair, not daring to respond or even to move. The rest of the shop was deadly silent for a long moment. Not another word passed between us.

From that day to this, I have asked myself, *Why didn't you just walk out? Why did you let him mistreat you that way?* All I can say is that, at that time, at that moment, I just couldn't. What really galls me? I tipped him!

Do you have a relationship that gives away too much power?

Perceptions

— :: —

The reality of life is that your perceptions—right or wrong—influence everything else you do.

—Roger Birkman

As a psychotherapist, when I read these words I think, of course, of cognitive behavioral therapy. This is a therapy that focuses on how you perceive things and what meanings you give to them—how you think about them—and thus, how you behave and feel. It helps you adjust perceptions and thinking that are not serving you well.

Birkman, who is also a psychologist, goes on to say: "When you get a proper perspective of your perceptions, you may be surprised how many other things fall into place."

For example, I had a client who consistently thought about other people as enemies, as people who did not like her, even, at times, that they were out to get her. These were the automatic categories into which she put other people. Cognitive therapy does not worry so much about how she got to this state of paranoia, but concerns itself with how she can change to more reality-based perceptions.

Her therapy consisted of looking in specific detail at what she assumed about others and how accurate it was. As she came to understand that her assumptions were not accurate—that her thinking about people was often not correct—she changed her behavior. Oversimplified of course, but that's basically how it works.

I am always giving myself a little cognitive behavioral therapy. (I know, I know, you should never shrink yourself!) It consists of simple questions: Am I thinking about this (person, situation, event, challenge, etc.) accurately? Why might I not be? What has influenced my perceptions?

And you? Is there anything in your life giving you some trouble? Can you see changing your thinking about it to a more accurate interpretation?

Consider for a moment . . . .

Beginner's Mind

— :: —

In the beginner's mind there are many possibilities,
but in the expert's mind there are few.

—Shunryu Suzuki

It takes a lot of experience to have a beginner's mind.
True experts—let's call them beginner-experts—have
traveled many roads, learned many skills, made numerous mistakes, and come back to the beginning, to start
again. True beginner-experts have done this many times.
Beginner-experts:

➤ Do not bring to a problem a limited number of
categories, into one of which they place the current one.

➤ Don't like the word "expert." It sets up unfair and
unrealistic expectations for all. Yet we use the word
and find it useful; and will continue to do so.

➤ See that they can easily be mistaken because they
have been mistaken before, and will be again.

➤ Are aware only of possibilities. The ways that open
before them are wide and long and numerous and
often exciting.

➤ Value their sense of observation and awareness as much as anything. They will not miss the broad strokes of brilliance, nor get distracted in myriad details.

➤ Are seekers. They are lovers. The have new eyes every time.

➤ Have learned to expect the unexpected. It does not surprise them, or rarely.

Little children are like beginners. The only difference between child-beginners and adult-beginners is that the children don't know that they don't know.

It is hard to begin a task that you have done many times and still have a beginner's mind. It is very hard. Other people are seldom helpful in this process. They want you to be the expert. They will call you expert and believe it.

Today, bring a "beginner's mind" to your daily tasks.

Directions of Our Lives

—— :: ——

Thank God, the ol' boy left.

—My uncle

Yes, that's what I heard my uncle say about his father, my maternal grandfather, who left his home in Ireland in 1885 as a young man to come to America. The occasion of the remark was a discussion of "the Troubles" in (now) Northern Ireland, where my grandfather was born in a village near the city of Derry (or Londonderry, depending on who's talking). In those days, all of Ireland was one country. My uncle was obviously happy not to have been born into what became, for a time, a violent and dangerous place with very limited opportunities for young, ambitious lads.

How different my own life would have been had "the 'ol boy" not left "the 'ol sod" and crossed the ocean to the New World. I wouldn't be here.

It makes me consider how frequently events that seem accidental or casual or totally out of our control profoundly influence the course of our lives. Even though we live with, and diligently foster, the fiction of having control over the direction of our lives, much of the time we don't really have it.

And that makes me think that so many of what we have considered our "moral failings"—not making enough money, not marrying well, not having the children we expected, not being smart enough, not having enough friends, not loving our work, not being as successful as we wanted or thought we should be or our parents thought we should be, or. . . Ah, the list is endless—are almost never moral failings.

Surely then, the important question is not so much what directions our lives have taken, but what have we done, and what do we continue to do, with what we've got to this point? Where is the opening through which I can contribute my own direction, my own desires, my own dreams? That's where to focus my energy, however broad or narrow that opening. That's where new life, uniquely mine, can gain purchase and grow into something beautiful. It's a grand opportunity.

('Tis.)

Within

— :: —

O pure people who wander the world,
amazed at the idols you see,
what you are searching for out there,
if you look within, you yourself are it.

—Rumi

Of all the common teachings of the world's religions and spiritual masters, this, I think, is the most basic. In searching for what is most important in human life, you must look within yourself. Rumi, a 13th-century Islamic saint and poet, expresses that idea poetically above.

Thus, the idea is nothing new. Certainly anyone with the least exposure to spiritual practice will have known this truth and assented to it heartily.

And yet . . . .

We keep wandering off the track and need to be reminded—which, of course, is consummately human. We are, as the poet says, truly "amazed at the idols" we see out there, simply because they are truly amazing: incredible riches, exotic and erotic pleasures, simple indulgences, palaces and pleasure domes, compelling beauty, personal and corporate power, unceasing acquisition, and so on. We know "the idols," don't we, you and I? And, of course, it seems much easier (or is it just more safe?) to look into the lives and souls of those around us rather than into our own.

But Rumi addresses us as "pure people," thus hinting at our basic innocence, pointing to a fundamental fact of our human nature. It is natural for us to be dazzled! The pleasures of the world, both the natural and the manufactured, are designed to please us.

So our saints and our spiritual teachers (do you ever consider that you might fit into either of those categories?) continue to remind those who will hear: First and last: Look in! "You yourself are it!"

In your game of "tag" this week, remember "you're it!"

Stretching

— :: —

*Man's mind stretched to a new idea never goes back
to its original dimensions.*

—Gerald Holton

I discovered the great benefits of stretching my body sometime in my forties. The benefits of this are abundant and almost immediate. One of them is that I just plain feel better after some yoga exercises or simply some stretches.

Stretching the mind is something else. Holton, a Harvard physicist, makes the point that, unlike the body, the mind once stretched never goes back to where it was. If I miss doing yoga for a week, stiffness gradually returns. If I am pushed intellectually to a new dimension, my frontier holds.

I like that idea.

I have been pushed many times. I remember one time in particular, when I was in graduate school. We were doing a case study in a psychology class. We were supposed to analyze the presenting symptoms and then make a diagnosis, which was something, at that time, that I philosophically resisted. I was convinced that too much diagnosis only helped insurance companies and too often limited the treatment of the patient. To cut to the chase, the professor became irritated with me for not being able to see the importance of diagnosis and how, in fact, it led to an even more specific, and thus improved, treatment.

I was having none of it, because I could not see beyond my own preconceived convictions. I was not open to the connections and sequences that the teacher and the rest of the class seemed to grasp so clearly. I was embarrassed and somewhat confused.

It came to me as I sat alone at my desk concentrating on my resistance. My mind, at that moment, stretched. I hope it has not slipped back from that point, but has kept expanding in an ever-widening direction.

There is, after all, a difference between a broad mind and a thick head.

Watch for opportunities to stre-e-e-etch. It makes you leaner in the body and broader in the mind.

The Brain

— :: —

We only use 10 percent of our brain.

—Urban myth

This is a saying that became popular several years ago, and is still heard. It claims that most human beings typically use only a fraction of their brain, and the rest lies fallow and uncultivated. My position on this statement is clear: I don't accept it. There is no scientific evidence to suggest that it is true. And the physiology of the human brain does not lend itself to such an interpretation of its use. We all use all of our brain.

The more interesting question, to me, is why does this myth persist? The popular culture seems to hold values that encourage us to want to believe it. What are they?

I suggest that what the 10-percent myth attempts to articulate is this: Many of us are under-challenged, or lazy, or have stopped caring about what we do. Consider:

➤ Many of us work at jobs that are not challenging or that keep us in an intellectual rut.

➤ Laziness is an inherent human characteristic.

➤ Often, we don't have to use all our intellectual capacity, so we don't. It's not laziness so much as apathy.

➤ Boredom is rampant.

➤ It's spiritually hard to care about your work if you're bored or philosophically alien to it.

I've personally had experiences with most of the above, with unfortunate or embarrassing results. But let's not blame my brain.

Wake up to the realities that underlie the 10-percent myth and how they affect your life. Are you under-challenged? Too often and inappropriately lazy? Apathetic or simply lacking interest in the world? Under-performing? Bored? Have you stopped caring? None of the above?

What's going on in your brain?

Looking

— :: —

Let us not look back in anger or forward in fear,
but around in awareness.

—James Thurber

I think Thurber, a 20th-century humorist, is really on to something here. Looking back in anger? So easy to do. Blaming myself or others? Somebody's got to take the blame; it's got to be somebody's fault. Dwelling on the past gives me a certain fulfillment—if only I had done this or that differently, if only someone had not been in the way, had not thwarted my efforts. It is a feeling that fills me up and takes care of an emptiness that might otherwise be there. I didn't get the breaks— such regret . . . things could have been different . . . if only, if only, if only. Dead end.

Looking forward in fear? Who knows what awaits me. There may be a total mess around the corner— look what happened to the neighbors; the same thing could happen to us; you can never tell. Worrying about the future really takes up a lot of my time and gives me something to occupy my mind. The situation in the world only gets worse and it seems no one can really do anything about it. And what if our leaders really are lying to us, then where are we? What if? What if? What if? Dead end.

Looking around in awareness? I see the building next door—gray and white, with dark-green and yellow bushes in front. There is a small view of the hills beyond the city, still golden but turning green with the rain now starting. I hear the soft hum of the fan on the shelf creating a cooling breeze on a warm autumn afternoon. In the hall, footsteps, and dog steps along with them, someone and their dog going or coming. Squeaky brakes from the parking lot below as someone arrives. Sunlight, low in the sky this time of year, comes in the window at an angle and makes shadows on the wall and on me. Presence . . . here . . . now. Breathe in; breathe out. Breathe in; breathe out. Breathe in; breathe out. Opening. And joy.

> *Thurber was a humorist. He knew how to take things lightly.*

Playing (Without Comment)

— :: —

It takes courage to play in a world that does not play.

—Fred Donaldson, American author

To live is to play at the meaning of life. . . . The upshot of this. . . is that it teaches us once and for all that childlike foolishness is the calling of mature men.

—Ernest Becker, American anthropologist

I seem to have been only like a boy playing on the seashore, and diverting myself in now and then finding a smoother pebble or a prettier shell, whilst the great ocean of truth lay all undiscovered before me.

—Isaac Newton, 17th-century physicist

We don't stop playing because we turn old, but turn old because we stop playing.

—George Bernard Shaw, Irish playwright

Man is most nearly himself when he achieves the seriousness of a child at play.

—Heraclitus, 6th-century B.C.E. philosopher

Necessity may be the mother of invention, but play is certainly the father.

—Roger von Oech, American author

There is a mystic in every one of us, yearning again to play in the universe.

—Matthew Fox, priest

The comic spirit masquerades in all things we say and do. We are each a clown and do not need to put on a white face.

—James Hillman, psychologist

Play is the exaltation of the possible.

—Martin Buber, 20th-century philosopher

You can discover more about a person in an hour of play than in a year of conversation.

—Plato, 5th-century B.C.E. philosopher

Play is the only way the highest intelligence of human-kind can unfold.

—Joseph Chilton Pearce, American author

And forget not that the earth delights to feel your bare feet and the winds long to play with your hair.

—Kahlil Gibran, poet

Big Enough World

— :: —

What should I do in a world that's not big enough to include me as I am?
Create a world that's big enough for all of you.

— Rita Blaney paraphrasing Phil Hall

Once upon a time, there was a little girl. She was a very good and obedient little girl. She was also very intelligent, exceptionally so, but she never thought about that, so she didn't know it.

She was interested in everything and everyone and learned new things every day. She loved animals, nature, and her friends, and spent as much time as she could with all of them.

She also loved her family. She was generous and open to all that life brought her every day. She was happy little girl.

Then she went to school.

Then she went to market.

Then she went to church.

Then she went to work.

Then she got married and had children.

Then she reached middle life.

Then she remembered that she used to be a happy little girl and wondered what happened.

Well, life happened, I guess. I mean, isn't this the story for so many of us? We really don't seem to "get it" until we're around forty and, by that time, it feels as if it's too late to do anything about it.

But it is not too late. That is the primary, but difficult, idea to comprehend. It's not too late to make your life "bigger." Indeed, I believe it is extremely difficult to "get it" before mid life, given the way our culture extends childhood and adolescence, and delays adulthood.

No, we're not all unhappy! No, we don't all want to get out of our lives! No, we don't all think we've made a mess of it! But I believe many of us experience at least some of these feelings from time to time—some of us more than others.

Awaken to your child. Spend some time thinking back to that little you, that young you, that wonderful, bright, interested, out-going you. Use your imagination to get back into the heart and soul of that little person. What expectations did that child have? What hopes? What would that child want?

A bigger world, no doubt.

Make your world bigger! Find ways.
Of course you can.

Asleep or Awake?

— :: —

How can you prove whether at this moment we are sleeping, and all our thoughts are a dream; or whether we are awake, and talking to one another in the waking state?

—Plato

You can't. At least, I don't think you can actually prove it. It does make for interesting reverie, though not a greatly practical one.

A more approachable, less theoretical question might be: How is it that, when we are quite sure that we are wide awake, in this moment and in this place—right now for example—we can, at the same time, be "asleep" to so much of what is going on in our lives, so much that is influencing us in the moment?

This is a central question of this entire book—one that is, in some way, related to all of its individual reflections.

It is also, I believe, the central question of our time. Ours is an age in which, at least in the Western world, relatively few live under threat of physical attack or violence, while many live comfortably and safely. Thus our challenge is not to allow ourselves to be lulled into sleep by a manic and stilted culture. Nor into silence and avoidance. Nor into burying our collective head in the sand. Nor into looking the other way because "it doesn't involve us." Nor into seeming to be awake yet being asleep to so much.

It may also be the central paradox for the Western world that, in achieving so much strength and security, we are made weak. Our accomplishments carry within them the seeds of our failure. Even the outrage of horrific terrorist attacks passes by the majority of us. We register them, but then slip back into waking sleep.

Most of us, I think, associate mainly with others who look like us, act like us, and basically agree with us. We avoid those who ruffle our feathers and raise the hard questions, or who feel a responsibility to react to the needs of people.

Well, when the times themselves conspire to lull us into forgetfulness, when the times themselves don't ruffle our feathers, we somehow have to find a way of ruffling each other's!

(Ruffle, ruffle.)

CHAPTER 10

Love and Family

—: ::—

Family and Work

I have frequently been questioned, especially by women, of how I could reconcile family life with a scientific career. Well, it has not been easy.

—Marie Curie

That was in the early 1900s. If it wasn't easy then, is it now? As a working woman and mother, Madame Curie was out of step with most of her contemporaries. Now, the working woman and mother is more the rule than the exception, and it's still not easy. And notice, Madame Curie did not really answer the question.

When I was quite a young boy, I clearly remember my father saying to me: "You have to work just as hard at family life as you do at your work life—maybe harder." At the time, I thought it was an odd thing to say and I didn't really get it.

In the early 21st century, balancing work life with private and family life is one of the most significant cultural challenges we face. Many people suffer from the difficulties that arise when they try and fail to integrate the two realms of work and home. What's a body to do?

Take some concrete steps to alleviate the tension. Here are some beginning thoughts for action:

➤ Begin by talking about it with your family (however you define family), or with your spouse or partner. Acknowledging a problem is always a good beginning. It is good for children to know their parents are concerned about creating a peaceful and caring home in which there is time for each other. They often come up with some good ideas, too.

➤ Carve out (even the term reveals the difficulty) some time for all (or both) of you to spend together every week. Yes, you can do that! You may have to cut out something.

➤ Consider the implications of your present priorities. Many a working person has changed his or her work to accommodate higher values. Is this something you can consider?

Work/Home: How's the balance for you?

Things

— :: —

If you want to see what children can do, you must stop giving them things.

—Norman Douglas

Spoiled children have been around ever since people started having children. Personally, I believe you can never give a child too much. In fact, we should give them as much as we possibly can. The question is not whether we should give to our children—or even how much. The question is what we should give. Douglas, a 19th-century writer, says we must stop giving them things if we want to foster creativity, usefulness, resourcefulness, and thus a chance at happiness. I couldn't agree more.

An overabundance of things—consumer goods, electronic gadgets, big-box items, gear, and stuff—threatens to ruin our children. It can hinder them from going inward, from accessing their inner lives and creating what they and their world need.

I have to acknowledge that, although I speak about parenthood, this is a portal though which I have not passed. I have no children and thus have no hands-on, the-buck-stops-here experience raising them. My only credentials are that I like children and tend to get along with them. And I have dealt with innumerable children as teacher, minister, and counselor. Unfortunately, I have seen too many of them damaged by having too many things.

The worst consequence is a killing off of an inborn inclination or instinct to develop an inner life—a life of imagination, of creativity, of generosity, of virtue, of spirituality, and, in the end, of love. Once we have what we actually need, the other things we possess hold only promises that eternally fail us. Our excess "things" never deliver as expected. Having too many things is seductive, fun, compelling, exciting—and ultimately boring.

Instead, give your children a super-abundance of your time, care, attention, company, skills, and interests.

Would I be so glib if I had children of my own and had to deal, day in and day out, with the immense cultural pressure to buy them more and more stuff? I don't know.

What I do know is that having too many things—bright, shiny, interesting things—tends to become an external distraction from the work of developing character and creativity. It always has been and it always will be.

Kids and things: seek a balance.

Private or Secret?

— :: —

If we all talked honestly about what's really happening in our sex lives, we'd realize that we're all normal because it's going to be about diversity.

—Betty Dodson

Is it desirable that we all talk honestly, in appropriate circumstances of course, about our sex lives? Yes, I think so. Our sex lives are basically private and should be shared at our discretion. That does not mean that they should be secret. My own sex life was once very secret; now it's private. Here's the way I understand the difference.

When something is private, it means that we can admit only those we want to admit. It also implies that the door is capable of being opened, whether or not we open it, and whether we open it to one, or to several— or to no one. Your sex life—what you do or don't do, what you like and don't like—should always be accessible. Don't barricade this part of yourself off somewhere (in a closet, for example). You should be able to speak about it appropriately to your spouse, for example, or to your therapist, or, on issues touching matters of health, to a health-care worker. The dominant emotions that stand at the door of privacy are confidence and serenity.

Secrecy is different. When something is secret, it is kept under lock and key, and there is only one key that is kept in the exclusive possession of the secret's owner. This is not a door that is capable of being opened. It is kept permanently locked. You are not able to talk honestly about what's behind it to anyone. The dominant emotions guarding the vault of secrecy are shame and fear.

Those who live a secret life will find immense relief when they exchange it for a private one. I know.

People whose work it is to understand our sexual lives—physicians, therapists, and clergy —all tell us versions of the same thing. When it comes to sex, diversity is the rule. Many loving couples have no "sex" at all; some old people have a lot more sex than you may think. It's no secret, it's just private.

Do you share honestly, appropriately?

Women and Men I

— :: —

A man's brain has a more difficult time shifting from thinking to feeling than a woman's brain does.

—Barbara de Angelis

And, for that matter, it is also more difficult for a man to shift back again from feeling to thinking. The male brain is well adapted to many tasks—linear thinking and problem solving for example—but it simply is not wired as well as a woman's brain for moving easily back and forth between feelings and thoughts.

This explains the feeling of ineptness that many men get when they are in an argument or even a discussion with a woman. As she easily darts back and forth between anger, reason, laughter, implications, surprise, earnestness, and so on, we men sometimes—although, not always—lumber along trying to think things through and feeling overwhelmed. If we do manage to get to our feelings, they often seem messy and out of our control. And, unfortunately, the typical male response is to quit the conversation, to bale out. I have certainly done it myself.

This is perhaps a bit exaggerated, but not too much, really. It is clear from current and responsible research that the brains of men and women are quite different in how they access and express feelings and thoughts. Each is adapted to different tasks.

Being aware and awake to this difference can be very important in your dealings with the opposite sex. Your expectations need to change so you can accommodate others. Typical and unhelpful responses are: "I never know what he's feeling!" and "I don't think she has a logical thought in her head!"

If both women and men take this difference into consideration and make the necessary adjustments, requests, and adaptations, the world will operate much more smoothly and with far fewer misunderstandings.

Make your adjustments. Help someone else do the same.

Women and Men II

— :: —

The test of a man is how well he is able to feel about what he thinks. The test of a woman is how well she is able to think about what she feels.

—Mary McDowell

The differences and similarities between men and women will always be a hot topic for discussion—and, in practice, for heated arguments. Perhaps that is because the causes and influences of those characteristics are both innate and cultural.

Here are some general characteristics I see of the differences between men and women in the expression of emotions:

➤ Men tend to be aggressive and competitive, and to express independence, favoring what some see as the "typically masculine" approach. Women favor more passive and cooperative feelings, with gentle expression that emphasizes connectedness.

➤ Men frequently like to be literal; women favor the symbolic. Thus, they often miss each other's emotional signals.

> Women favor emotion as a motive for acting; men favor logic.

> Men often get to an emotion by way of thought; their first response to anything is likely to be to think about it. Feeling follows. Women tend to respond to life directly with feelings.

> Women often prefer to express an emotion verbally, by talking about it and around it. Men often prefer to express what they are feeling through action, like enjoying an activity together.

> Men typically express feelings infrequently, leading some to wrongly think that men don't have feelings. Women typically express feelings more often.

And now, an important caution. Do you see the problem here? For every one of those suggested differences (stereotypes, in a way), you and I both know people in whom the characteristics are very different, even reversed. This, of course, is perfectly normal and healthy. Stereotypes are oversimplified and uncritical. Naming some of the general differences, however, can help awaken a new understanding between men and women.

> *Today: Think about your feelings.*
> *Feel what you think.*

Women and Men III

— :: —

Women need a reason to have sex. Men just need a place.

    —Billy Crystal

Do you seriously expect me to be the first Prince of Wales in history not to have a mistress?

    —Prince Charles

There were three of us in this marriage, so it was a bit crowded.

    —Diana, Princess of Wales

One of the significant issues between men and women, obviously, is the attitudes and assumptions they each have about sex. Often these conjoin harmoniously; often, too, they do not.

Begin with the expressions above. Diana's is metaphoric, softly but clearly expressed with a sense of decorum and wit. Billy and Charlie, also with wit, simply state—the prince uses a rhetorical question—what they intend for you to know.

However, I believe the most significant challenge for men and women to understand about each other on this issue is for both to accept that men are more able and willing to separate the acts of sex from the acts of love and commitment. Women are more able and willing to unite them. Is this attitude based on the ancient-but-constantly-changing roles of hunter/homemaker? One has the value of propagating the species; the other of safe-guarding and nurturing it?

Whatever the differences between men and women—and in particular between *this* man and *this* woman—I believe that keeping in mind these innate differences will add light rather than heat to the process. Not for the purpose of defending a moral position, nor for making an excuse for one, but simply for recognizing the differing natures we have been given.

Whew! Did I negotiate carefully enough through that mine-field while still adding some value to the issue?

(I'm not sure he did.)

What's a Family?

—— :: ——

Family isn't about whose blood you have. It's about who you care about.

—Trey Parker and Matt Stone

Have you ever watched *South Park* on TV? Its writers (Parker and Stone) exempt nothing—nothing!—from their searing humor. They are definitely irreverent. They skewer liberals and conservatives alike, but always with a degree of empathy and nuance. That is a considerable achievement for a cartoon. It is also more sophisticated and challenging than it may seem at first. Unfortunately, many people can't get by the parody and cynicism to appreciate the frequent gems of insight, like the one above: family is who you care about.

Maybe only people who have experienced a non-traditional family can make such a statement—perhaps especially those who have been rejected by their natural families and accepted by other caring families.

Certainly, there are many natural families that don't act toward each other as families should—with love, kindness, and care. Indeed, in some families, the members don't even seem to know each other.

Those of us who can say "I was born into a great family!" are uniquely blessed. Yes, we have our problems and our feuds; yes, we have our disagreements, disloyalties, and mistakes. But in the end, as one observer said of my natural family, "All in all, you guys do seem basically to like each other."

I like to speak of "family who are friends," like siblings and cousins, and "friends who are family," those with whom bonds of friendship go deep and are lasting.

My natural family, a vast Hungarian-Irish-German throng, live for the most part on the other side of the country—unfortunately for me. Thus my "friends who are family" are especially important to me. When we get together, generally in one of our homes around a groaning board, someone inevitably gives a bless . . . I mean makes a toast:

"A la famiglia!"

Unfair!

—::—

The great advantage of living in a large family is that early lesson of life's essential unfairness.

—Nancy Mitford

As the youngest of four with lots of close cousins, I know Nancy Mitford's right. And it's a very useful lesson to learn, too. Perhaps it is even the most useful lesson of all: Life is not fair. To make peace with that lesson, no matter how early you learn it, takes the better part of a lifetime.

In *Our Town*, one of Wilder's characters says, "we try to have the unkind and the mean sink to the bottom and the virtuous and thoughtful rise to the top, but so far haven't be able to manage it." Perhaps the most significant benefit of knowing this basic fact of human existence is that you stop wasting an immense amount of time fretting over unfairness.

My most recent bout with unfairness came from a close friend's application for work. It was clear, not just to friends, but even (admittedly!) to the employer, that my friend was the person best qualified for the position. He was not hired because of a complicated combination of company politics and regulations. It was "wrong"; it was "unfair"; it was not what I wanted!

Soon after that, I attended a fund-raiser for a member of Congress who was subjected to a rant by a constituent about how the then-current president had "stolen" the election. He cut them off, saying "That's over and done. Focus on what we have ahead of us!" These are the words of a politically savvy and effective legislator—one who has learned the lesson of unfairness.

Awaken and become specifically aware of the unfair situations in your own life, whether they are long-term or something that happened only yesterday.

Why waste time on something you can't change?

Your Choice

—— :: ——

When did you decide to be straight?

—Sally Eastman

I'm writing, in this particular piece, to heterosexual readers (but LGBTQ readers: don't stop). No one decides his or her sexual orientation. There are a small percentage of people who claim to have made the choice; who am I to judge them wrong? However, it remains an area of murky truth and changeable findings difficult to pin down.

Even though 50 percent of Americans believe sexual orientation is not a choice, 11 percent still say it is a conscious choice. Thirty-four percent believe it's a combination of both the person's choice and the person's inborn nature. The majority of the 45 percent (34 plus 11) are almost certainly persuaded by a particular brand of religious conviction.

Why would anyone choose to be gay or lesbian, bisexual or transgender given the attitudes toward us in our culture? It makes no sense, especially when you think of the fact that the "decision" would most commonly be made during adolescence, a time one wants only to conform, fit in. And, even if it *were* a choice, why shouldn't people be free to make that choice?

So now to the question posed in the title. If sexual orientation *was* in fact a choice you made, when did *you* decide to be straight? At what age did it happen? Did you discuss it with your parents or teachers? Have you ever considered changing it? Did you give careful consideration to the other options? Was it a close call for you? What influenced you to make the choice you did, that is to be heterosexual? Get it?

When will we realize that the determination of our sexual orientation (and sexual identity too)— although still not completely understood—is largely pre-determined and that people come in all sexual varieties: hetero-, homo-, bi-, trans-, and queer. In addition, they can be asexual and hypersexual, celibate or very active, and so on.

While duality is what's acceptable, variety is what is real.

> *Do you need to wake up about this?*
> *What is your choice?*

Kissing and Talking

— :: —

Don't have sex, man. It leads to kissing and pretty soon you have to start talking.

—Steve Martin

You can choose to talk about sex, or not—or land somewhere in between. I make my stance clear from the beginning: Of course we need to talk about sex! Why wouldn't we? Why would we select one of the most significant aspects of human life and surround it with a silence that perpetuates ignorance and untold suffering?

It makes no sense not to talk about sex. But that is, for the most part, what we do. Naturally, there are reasons—the biggest one being shame. But habit, ignorance, embarrassment, and laziness all add to the pressure to keep sex in the dark.

It's time to wake up.

Comedian Steve Martin's stereotypically male attitude above may bring a chuckle, but it will not bring sanity.

Talk to your children about sex. Start early and appropriately, and continue for as long as necessary. If you're not already there, get over the idea that talking about sex to young people "gives them ideas" they're better off without. Believe me, they already have them! They're built-in. What young people need is wisdom, understanding, and knowledge.

Have a conversation with your husband/wife/ spouse/partner about sex. Tell each other what you think, what you feel, what you like.

Be the kind of adult (parent, teacher, or other) who is approachable about the topic of sexuality.

It is quite possible to talk to anyone about all aspects of human sexuality while respecting any religious or moral convictions they or you may hold. Of course. The question is: Why wouldn't that be possible?

Soon. Talk to someone honestly about sex.

Truth or Fear?

— :: —

Nature chooses who will be transgender; individuals don't choose this.

—Mercedes Ruehl, American actress

No person is your friend who demands your silence or denies your right to grow.

—Alice Walker, author and activist

Not everyone is meant to make a difference; but for me, the choice to live an ordinary life is no longer an option.

—Spider Man, comic-book character

For my thoughts are not your thoughts, neither are your ways my ways.

—Isaiah 55:8

So long as you are still worried about what others think of you, you are owned by them. Only when you require no approval from outside yourself can you own yourself.

—Neale Donald Walsch, American author

We know what we are,
but know not what we may become.

—William Shakespeare, English playwright

I am convinced that the only people worthy of consideration in this world are the unusual ones. For the common folk are like leaves of a tree, and live and die unnoticed.

—Frank L. Baum, *The Scarecrow of Oz*

A transgender person is someone whose gender identity differs from the gender identity of their physical sex as assigned at birth. Transgender people are born transgender and have no choice in this aspect of who they are. There have always been transgender people. This is the reality—but the world is slow indeed to catch up with it. So much suffering must be endured before these truths will be accepted and blessed along with all the other truths in the world. What is your attitude toward transgender people?

Your choice: Truth or fear.

Celibacy

—::—

Give me chastity and continence—but not yet.

—St. Augustine

No matter your opinion of Augustine, his glib comment on sex remains provocative, especially coming from a fourth-century saint.

But, words often have confusing meanings. Chastity can mean abstention from (morally) unpermitted sex, or from sex altogether. Continence can mean more or less the same thing, but comes down on the side of complete avoidance.

Put them together as Augustine does, and what you have is celibacy. Picture the young Augustine facing a life of celibacy and uttering this prayer. Literally, celibacy means refraining from marriage, with the added religious dimension of nothing overtly sexual going on at all.

I lived celibate for a good number of years. I don't recommend it as an imposed state of being.

Certainly, there are people who live healthy, celibate lives; I know some who freely and maturely choose it. I can also appreciate that celibacy can liberate certain unusual individuals and help focus their human energy into a life of service. However, I believe that, for the vast majority, celibacy does not foster healthy human life.

For one thing, in most people, imposed celibacy leads to obsession with (and too often, compulsion about) that which is forbidden. For another, celibacy is probably kept in the breach as much as in the observance.

We need to leave behind our negative assumptions about sex. We need to awaken to the fact that sex is a good and natural thing. The negative energy that surrounds sex in our culture—what I call sex-negativity—is amazingly destructive. It creates disabling obsessions and addictions, self-loathing, impossible demands, double lives, and much more.

Add to that the general embarrassment that the subject evokes, the shame it calls forth, and our avoidance of the subject for fear of being branded as abnormal or indecent because of our "excessive" interest.

How did we get so wrong-headed?

Will you do something soon to emphasize the beauty and goodness of human sex?

Out the Window

— :: —

*I was an altar boy, a spokesperson for the Virgin Mary,
I was a choir boy, but then at the age of 14, I discovered
masturbation and all that went out the window.*

—Guillermo del Toro

You're no doubt wondering *What in the world is he going to say about masturbation?* Well, my message is really
simple and in keeping with the theme of these reflections. I hope it is helpful. Masturbation is perhaps the
most commonly performed practice that no one talks
about, although that's slowly changing. It is an intensely
private practice that we rarely address in a public discussion. In fact, if you're upset about the topic appearing
here, I suspect that is precisely because it appears here.

Masturbation has never had a place in the public
discourse of the modern era. It was forbidden by religions—spilling seed and all that. My motive in addressing it here stems from my experience as a current
psychotherapist, a former clergyman, and a human being. I know from my work that masturbation results
in a huge amount of deep shame, and that that shame

can and does spill over into other personality areas like self-confidence and self-esteem. This can debilitate otherwise successful lives. There's no reason for that to happen in the 21st century. After all, says Woody Allen, adding a needed light note, don't knock masturbation; it's sex with someone I love!

Moreover, from what I have read, and from several frank conversations with women, I believe there is a significant difference between men and women in this area, as there is in all aspects of sexuality. To oversimplify, men do it more. Everyone masturbates at some time in their lives, although there are probably exceptions.

What we need to do is to get rid of the guilt and the shame. I think we should help children integrate masturbation as a natural part of human behavior. By taking it out of the shadows, we can keep it from becoming compulsive behavior and allow it to become a normal part of human life and conversation. I'm not saying masturbation should not be private. But let's acknowledge its existence without shame. Not to do so is harmful to many people, and just plain silly.

> *"The only thing about masturbation to be ashamed of is doing it badly" (Sigmund Freud).*

CHAPTER 11

The Ecosystem—aka Home

— :: —

One Moon

One moon shows in every pool;
in every pool the one moon.

— Zen Forest saying

The late evening rain has passed and, as darkness falls, the Full Moon rises. It is reflected, as brilliantly as in a mirror, by the pool that forms on the darkened street. It captures your attention and you stop simply to look at the Moon, in the pool and in the heavens. Your Moon.

A Vietnamese woman's eyes follow the silver line of moonlight across the river and then mount the sky to the Moon itself. She breathes deeply and pauses a moment in the gathering dusk on her way to the village. Her Moon.

A teenage boy walks with his family in the evening in Stockholm and looks out at the Moon rising over the harbor. Its clarity and beauty lead him to point and remark, "Look at the Moon!" His Moon.

An old man sitting with companions on the plains of Serengeti in the quiet of the evening wonders how many times in his long life he has looked at the Moon rise over the flooded plains, and if it ever looked more beautiful than tonight. His Moon.

In the Lake Country of Chile, an infant girl is carried by her mother down a quiet road to home. She cannot take her eyes off the brilliant Moon nor keep her hands from reaching for its reflection on the lake. She coos a message of desire. Her mother smiles. Their Moon.

All the pools of water in the world, oceans or puddles, reflect the same Moon. It belongs to all of us who see it reflected there for a transcendent moment—no matter who we are, no matter where we are.

The Moon belongs to us all.

(I wonder if we asked anyone's permission when we went there?)

> *Watch for the Moon reflected in water.*
> *Think of everyone in the world.*

Consumer Society

— :: —

America must be the teacher of democracy, not the advertiser of the consumer society. It is unrealistic for the rest of the world to reach the American living standard.

—Mikhail Gorbachev

➤ Tourist destinations are, as often as not, simply a large and beautifully laid out cluster of stores—upscale boutiques to be sure, but nevertheless stores with stuff to sell. People wander around, in and out of stores, buying things they probably don't need, and call it vacation.

➤ Compared to the rest of the world, the amount the United States consumes is mind-boggling.

➤ Our culture is ruled by the bottom line. By very definition, the bottom line is: Are we making money?

➤ The gap between the very rich and the poor is getting wider and wider. More and more consumption, but by whom?

➤ Our accelerating consumption does not seem to be making us happier.

It's this last observation I want to emphasize. Consuming, by definition, means "getting stuff," filling ourselves and our homes with "things." Who are we trying to satisfy? What are we trying to fulfill, to achieve? Whatever it is, and however noble our desires, it does not seem to be working.

Let's begin by doing our bit to lower consumption and raise up democracy! Let's think twice before we buy something we don't need and that we know, if we're honest, we will eventually throw out. Let's replace the desire to acquire with a desire to do something more lasting, more in line with the needs of the world, and more fulfilling to us. Write a letter to a friend? Give the gift of a visit? Volunteer for an hour? Donate to a cause? Join a Green group? Endless possibilities without taxing the imagination.

Let's leave the stuff we don't need in the stores.

Water

—::—

We have the purest water supply in the world, and yet we buy billions of bottles of the stuff!

—Gary Trudeau

That quote is from the comic strip "Doonesbury," and it's true; I checked it out. America, wake up about your drinking-water habits! Here are some facts to consider:

➤ The Earth Policy Institute (EPI) says global consumption of bottled water doubled between 1999 and 2004, reaching 41 billion gallons annually. Bottled water is often no healthier than tap water, but it can be 10,000 times more expensive. Some very large bottlers simply bottle tap water.

➤ At as much as $10 a gallon, bottled water costs more than twice as much as gasoline.

➤ The EPI report lists the United States as the world's biggest drinker of bottled water, consuming 7 billion gallons annually.

➤ Italians drink the most bottled water per person, equivalent to about two glasses a day. (It's a world-wide phenomenon.)

- More than 2.7 million tons of plastic are used to bottle water each year, according to EPI. The plastic most commonly used is polyethylene terepthalate (PET), which is derived from crude oil.

- Making bottles to meet Americans' demand for bottled water requires more than 1.5 million barrels of oil annually, enough to fuel some 100,000 cars for a year.

- About 86 percent of plastic water bottles in the United States become garbage or litter, according to the Container Recycling Institute in Washington, D.C.

In some countries where the water supply is poor, bottled water makes healthy sense. The bottled-water lobbies are big and have their side of the story; their Web sites are easy to find.

If you are looking for a clear, practical, and simple project that will put you on the road to ecological soundness and global health, here is one for you to begin right now. Replace your plastic-water-bottle habit with any reusable container filled with your perfectly healthy tap water. Or would you rather be a victim of marketing? The "Doonesbury" strip quoted above includes the following: "Bottled water is a triumph of perceived need over reason—the greatest marketing coup in history."

Wake up. Open the tap.

Pachamama

— :: —

The Symposium explores the link between three of humanity's most critical concerns: environmental sustainability, social justice, spiritual fulfillment.

—Awakening the Dreamer Symposium

To many people, "Pachamama" is just a funny word—at least when they first hear it. When they learn what's behind it, however, it becomes a wonderful word. I mean "wonderful" literally, as in "full of wonders."

I was introduced to Pachamama by a friend who invited me to attend the "Awakening the Dreamer Symposium," a short day's experience of initiation into the purpose and meaning of the Pachamama Alliance. I liked the Pachamama organization because I found it balanced and well-run. It includes both theory and practice. It offers many ways to participate and begin changing our collective reality. It operates in "both/and" terms, rather than "either/or" terms. Check it out at *www. pachamama.org*. The Web site also has links to groups that may better fit your interests and imagination.

The mission of the Pachamama Alliance is: "To preserve the Earth's tropical rainforests by empowering the indigenous people who are its natural custodians; to contribute to the creation of a new global vision of equity and sustainability for all." One of the group's compelling goals is "to change the dream of the North." Some cultures, like some in South America, still live in their traditional Earth-honoring ways. They refer to our modern worldview as our collective dream—the dream of the North—and they urge us, for the sake of all life, to change that dream. The Alliance values and brings together the skills and knowledge of the North and the skills and knowledge of the South. This grabbed my attention as a goal I thought I could support enthusiastically and completely.

If you think saving the rainforest is just another do-gooder cause; if you think sustainability is hopeless or unimportant or arbitrary; if you think that it is impossible to change the dream of the North; if you think these objectives are optional—*wake up!*

I believe it is important to associate ourselves with a responsible group that is seeking a "new vision," a "new dream," and a new way to be on our Earth.

> *Determine your practical response to this challenge. If you're already involved, how can you deepen that involvement?*

Changing Your Dream

— :: —

It is as if we are living inside of a dream, sleepwalking toward oblivion.

—Pachamama Alliance

What comes to your mind when you say "Live the American dream!" The typical dream that most of us articulate and that many of us actually live has to change. It's not sustainable; it's not socially just. And, for most, it's not spiritually fulfilling. This is one of the messages of the Pachamama Alliance.

The dream we are collectively dreaming right now is like "sleepwalking toward oblivion, while self-serving, shortsighted interests encourage our slumber with managed news, a celebrity culture, and other weapons of mass distraction."

Pachamama tells us that changing our collective dream will have to be a "do-it-yourself-together project." It will be accomplished by committed individuals working in concert—tens of millions of us, each willing to think and act in a whole new way. We'll accomplish this in community, or not at all.

The idea of community (rather than the individual) may, in fact, be a good place to start changing the dream. The villain in the play, the Alliance claims, is not Big Business, the corporate media, the military-industrial complex, or even those seeking personal profit. The villain is an *outmoded worldview*. Our institutions appear incapable of addressing the global crisis, precisely because they do not realize that they are looking at an interconnected unity through the lens of fragmentation and individualism.

The villain, in other words, is our collective dream!

Can we not say the same of our own outmoded worldviews? Of our own misguided dreams? To change our lives, we must change our dreams.

Change the dream! Change your dream!

The Car

—— :: ——

The car changed our dress, manners, social customs, vacation habits, the shape of our cities, consumer purchasing patterns, common tastes and positions in intercourse.

—T. D. Regehr

The car changed all of that—and much more besides. The car still determines a great deal of how we live our lives.

I live at the top of a long, steep hill. Every time I drive home, I am aware that, if I did not have a car, I probably would not live there. Neither would my neighbors. And if that were the case—if none of us had cars—surely there would be a public outcry demanding fast and efficient public transportation so we could live there.

Cars! Can't live with 'em (pollution, traffic congestion, cost, maintenance, parking); can't live without 'em (we simply could not get to many—most?—of the places we want to go). We're in a tough fix and it's long-term. When cars came on the scene, public transportation took a nose-dive from which it has never recovered.

Besides all that, we absolutely love our cars. Men, especially, identify with and enjoy their cars. They represent power, freedom, beauty, fun, and independence.

The hard and unwelcome truth, however, is that we have to wake up about cars. It can't go on, this steady and accelerating proliferation of gas-guzzling automobiles. Here is a good example of a free-market economy controlling the country more for its own profit rather than for the good of the country. From the very beginning, the automobile industry and its lobbies have been incredibly powerful and, as a rule, we have been a willingly receptive populace.

There are some good signs, however. There are more and more hybrid vehicles, at least where I live. Some of them are plug-in hybrids. Smaller. Less gas. Less expensive to operate. Kinder to the environment. Quieter. And more and more of us are taking public transportation. They're steps.

Will you take some step to be a sign of change?

All to Yourself

— :: —

I have my own sun and moon and stars, and a little world all to myself.

—Henry David Thoreau

This reflection is challenging for me to write and I will have to choose my words carefully in order to be honest. I want to look at Nature in the context of the tradition of individualism that is so strong in our country, especially compared to the tradition of community common in other national cultures—as in Asia and much of Europe, for instance.

On one hand, I totally relate to and appreciate Thoreau's words and his withdrawal to Walden. I have loved the wilderness my whole life and continue to seek the isolation and stillness that wilderness travel offers as often as I can. It has been a significant joy of my life.

On the other hand, I have begun to see the need for developing a deeper sense of community, of being and doing things together as a kind of family or a group that shares camaraderie and a sense of commonality.

I now see the negative aspects of withdrawal into my own private, personal, exclusive space and time as a symptom of a national challenge. I see the individualism that is deep in our history and practice as an attribute to be faced and transformed. As our population grows and our lives become more complex, as our natural resources are increasingly compromised and our destinies become increasingly interwoven, I begin to see that our strong individualistic tendencies need to be muted.

As wilderness access becomes more and more the privilege of the wealthy, can we afford to continue to honor and strive to emulate Thoreau's "little world all to myself"? Is our world already too small for that? Must we not rather introduce a new way to be in Nature? A way that brings us there together? Huge questions, these, and with no quick and easy resolutions—especially not for the likes of me. But I soldier on.

(This guy lives in another world! Get him help!)

Nature

—::—

Thoreau had the sun and sky to himself, but just let him try it in Yellowstone National Park on Memorial Day.

—Newsweek

A recent study, sponsored by the Nature Conservancy, reports that we are not getting out into nature as much as we used to and, significantly, that nature will not be cared for and protected if people stay away from it. To know it firsthand is to love it, the logic goes. And to love it is to protect it. I buy that argument, even though its counter-argument is significant: We are polluting and destroying the natural world by over-visiting it; indeed, there are many clear examples of this. So leave nature alone to heal itself.

In this context, it occurs to me that the wise people of every age keep in their hearts and practice what is best and beautiful from the past, while letting the rest go. They adapt and embrace the new, the innovative, and the true that confronts them daily. They have the finesse to recognize what is essential and what isn't.

This is the challenge in our relationship to the natural world. If the Nature Conservancy's study is correct—they blame the decline on video games and the Internet—then our lack of knowledge and commitment to the Earth comes at exactly the wrong time: global warming, polluted air and oceans, poisoned food, and so on.

One way to deal with the dismal scenario of an uncommitted citizenry confronting a degenerating Earth is with a two-stage plan:

➤ The logic behind the restorative-nature-of-Nature argument is sound. When you spend time at the beach, in the mountains, hiking a trail, visiting a park, floating on a river, paddling on a lake, surfing the ocean—well, you just feel better. Thus you love your time on the Earth. Thus you'll do something to show your love. Right?

➤ But responsible stewardship toward the places we visit is also essential. Stewardship implies responsibility and the realization that we are visitors here. Our commitment and pledge should be: Let our passing this way do no harm.

We can always hope!

Junk

— :: —

Junk is the ultimate merchandise. The junk merchant does not sell his product to the consumer, he sells the consumer to the product. He does not improve and simplify his merchandise, he degrades and simplifies the client.

—William S. Burroughs

I'll grant you Burroughs is not the most unimpeachable source. Nevertheless, I believe what he says here is accurate. In more contemporary language, you could say that the dealer in junk first creates the market, then produces the product to fill the "need." Brilliant, actually. It's difficult to deny that this practice is common in these days of advanced marketing strategies.

If this is so, we are all "simplified and degraded," manipulated by propaganda to feel a need that, before manipulation, we did not feel—all to enable someone to take our money. It seems to make no difference what the "product" is, what it's made of, or its effect on the environment. Will it make money for the merchant? That's all that counts.

It used to be that someone in the junk business actually dealt in real junk. There were junk yards. Now junk is in the stores masquerading as useful merchandise. Mega-stores are brimming with it.

And we buy it, tons of it. I know I have. Poorly made, practically useless, often unattractive and tacky, hyped beyond belief, bright and shiny—and next month in the trash.

Why do we do it? Because we've "been had" by skillful marketing experts who have "simplified and degraded" us to exactly the point at which we serve them. We've become the "consumer" sold to the "product." We've actually, truthfully come to think that we need this stuff. Or our kids think they need it because commercials have skillfully convinced them of it! Whew! Shame on us for being so distracted that we buy into all that!

Think about junk in your life.

As It Is

—::—

Everything
just as it is,
as it is,
as is.
Flowers in bloom.
Nothing to add.

      —Robert Aiken (Roshi)

How far we are, most of us, from living close to Nature. From living close to the Earth, the trees, the rocks and the seasons—and the moon!

How far we are from knowing, in our bones, that the sticks and the stones, the grains and the grass, the sand and the dirt are our bodies.

How far we live from swimming easily in the waters of the Earth—the rivers!—and from scrambling over the mountains and crossing the dry places and the wetlands, the moors and the plains.

How far, how far, how far!

Come closer, the Zen master invites us. Come and spend time on the Earth. See everything "just as it is."

Spend quiet time simply being upon the Earth as it is—that is, while it is and in exactly the situation in which it is. The Earth as is.

Contemplating the Earth as it is is worth your time.

It tells you who you are, whence you came, whither you go.

It calls your name, even gives you your name, if you are still enough to hear.

Flowers in bloom!

In the meadows and grasslands, in the parks and gardens of the cities, in the suburbs around the cities, on the less-traveled byways and hot-traveled freeways, along paths that lead through the dark forest and out again to the dunes of the ocean's coast, on trees and on plants and on hedges. Flowers in bloom.

Nothing to add. Nothing to add.

Now awake. You are complete.

Recycling

— :: —

*We are not to throw away those things which can
benefit our neighbor. Goods are called good because
they can be used for good: they are instruments for
good, in the hands of those who use them properly.*

—Clement of Alexandria

Do you recycle? Do you use the things you need and
then return them to new life? What you recycle will
have life again—and maybe even again and again.

Recycling is a specific way to express that you know
your place in the universe as a sojourner, as someone
who is traveling through for a while and then moves on.

➤ It is a sign that you care about what you leave to those
to come.

➤ It is a sign you comprehend—at least in some dark
way—your place in the cosmos and the effect that
your waste will have on it.

➤ It is a sign of your love for the world, for its wonders of
nature, of flora and fauna, of oceans and mountains and
deserts. And, as the first-century saint and philosopher
reminds us, it benefits our neighbors.

➤ It is a clear sign of what you believe about your Earth and how you treat her. It speaks of care and reverence and respect.

Recycle organic waste materials into compost, into the earth, into the soil, and thus into your food, into your body for growth and new life. Recycle paper and metal into new products useful to all the world.

The act of recycling makes you think about what you use and the amount you use, about what you really need and what you don't. It encourages the simplicity the world needs so desperately right now. Especially from the "greatest" consumer society. But no time for useless guilt, only for determined action.

In the end, our very selves, our bodies, will go back to the earth and we will become part of the eternal cycle of life and death and life and death and life . . .

> *Use it up, wear it out, make it do, or do without . . .*
> *but always recycle.*

One

— :: —

Lack of awareness of the basic unity of organism and environment is a serious and dangerous hallucination.

—Alan Wilson Watts

The current crisis of the world environment is a topic we have all heard about a great deal in recent years, from global warming to polluted water and air. It risks becoming a boring topic. There have been many excellent and deeply informed statements, warnings, and expressions of the crisis; I cannot really add anything. So I would like to emphasize two ideas.

First: I believe that an "awareness of the basic unity of organism and environment," in Alan Watts' happy phrase, is part of your spiritual life. Of course, it is also part of your intellectual, social, and economic lives. But most fundamentally, it is a spiritual reality. We all have a spiritual life, by which I mean the meanings and values by which we live. It is from that level, the spiritual level, that we are most motivated to act. You and I will only be motivated to respond to the global crisis by willingly giving time and money, making sacrifices and self-negations, changing living habits and assumptions about the good life, if the meanings and values by which we live move us to do so. Otherwise, forget it. This has huge implications for all religious organizations.

Second: I believe that the nay-sayers, at this advanced point in our understanding of the crisis, are motivated by fear or denial or both. Fear and denial have blocked the reality of the world's crisis from entering into their spiritual lives. This has tremendous implications for all the rest of us.

It is a time to stop and think about just what the basic unity of organism and environment means. Not to do so is a "dangerous hallucination." One is part of the other, comes from and returns to the other, is origin and home to the other. One is the other. One is one. One.

Take a "Green" step this week, whether your first or one of many.

CHAPTER 12

Day in and Day out

—— :: ——

Reading and the Internet

Some books are to be tasted, others to be swallowed, and some few to be chewed and digested.

—Francis Bacon

But first, they have to be opened—which is something many current pollsters tell us is not happening nearly as frequently as in the past. I heard a professor of college freshmen say that she has students who admit they never read an entire book. The usual culprit to get the blame is the Internet.

As one who has enjoyed a lifelong love affair with books, I am tempted to become upset and be critical of this cultural trend. Actually, my first sentiment is something like pity or sorrow for those who have not known the immense and varied benefits of book reading.

Is there anything like becoming so absorbed in a good book that everything fades away and you are transported into another world? Maybe that can happen in front of a screen; I don't know. It hasn't for me. But I admit I have never read a "book" on a computer. What's so different about reading words on a screen rather than on a page? I have a good friend who has read several books on his Blackberry. When I ask him why he reads on an electronic device and not from a "real" book, he just looks at me and asks "Why not?" Indeed!

Still, I have visions of people ten years from now reading these words and laughing, "Imagine, just ten years ago people were still reading hard-copies—whole texts!—and wondering why so few read them on screen! Ha, ha, ha!" I imagine the disappearance of libraries; I recall their stacks and the pleasure of browsing them; I mourn the decaying of old books with no new ones to replace them.

Is this simply an emotional attachment and an irrational fear? Is this one more step on my inevitable journey to becoming a curmudgeon, skulking about and complaining about how much better things used to be? Or is it a reasonable concern? I'm not sure.

(Will someone please help this guy think in a new way!)

Heretic or Prophet?

— :: —

All great truths begin as blasphemies.

—George Bernard Shaw

The clearest example I know of this is Galileo. First condemned as heretic (*It is impossible that the Earth is round!*); later honored as prophet (*Of course the Earth is round!*). Then there's Martin Luther, from disloyal and disobedient cleric (*Abuse in God's Church? Impossible!*) to revered leader of the Reformation (*Maybe we overlooked a few things!*). And Nelson Mandela, jailed for twenty-seven years as a dangerous traitor (*Of course apartheid is God's will!*) then a democratically elected liberator of South Africa (*Apartheid is simply institutionalized bigotry!*).

The difference between a nut-case and a hero is often simply time. The transformation happens on a smaller scale all the time. Let's bring it to the level of our lives. When I was not accepted into the graduate school of my choice (at the very last minute, all packed and ready to leave), I judged it a serious mistake on the part of the university and a complete personal disaster. I acted accordingly, causing a good deal of trouble for the administrator who thwarted my desire (*He blasphemes!*). In the end, the administrator was proved right in his judgment of my preparedness for the course for which I applied (*He was prophetic!*). Moreover, my rejection became a wonderfully pivotal event in my life, an event that led me to so much of what I now consider a blessing. I clearly did not take the long view. I didn't recognize that things are often not what they appear to be. I didn't try to find other ways of understanding what was happening.

Stop and think before you act! And then breathe deeply a few times. Do this for several days and maybe several weeks. Only then, begin to think about acting. All of this is, of course, so obvious—unless you don't stop and think. We can't be reminded too often.

Prophets often get stoned with the blocks they fashion. The prophet simply speaks the truth to anyone. That university administrator got more than one angry letter—may well have been called into someone's office and questioned. His decision to say no was based on what he considered fair, correct, and just—but it caused him some trouble. Prophets of all kinds are used to that.

What does prophecy look like from your point of view?

Living Words

—::—

A word is dead when it is said, some say.
I say it just begins to live that day.

    —Emily Dickinson

My own weakness is to *not* say something that needs to be said. I have oceans of regrets about things I didn't say. But I spend a good deal of time with my foot in my mouth as well.

The incident I recall most clearly, however, happened to a friend. Four of us were invited to dinner at the home of another friend. Unknown to us, she had also invited her daughter and son-in-law to join us.

The evening was memorable for many reasons, not the least of which was the quirky personality of our hostess. While we were at dinner, one of my acquaintances was speaking about his work. In the course of his conversation, he mentioned that he often spoke on the phone with real estate professionals in New York City who were Jewish. He laughingly mentioned that he and his co-workers referred to them as "the 212s"—a reference to their telephone area code. It was clearly an indelicate remark that everyone let pass; well not everyone.

Later in the meal, I asked our hostess' son-in-law, who had been quiet during most of the evening, to tell us something about himself—where he was from, his work, and so on. He immediately answered, in a voice loud enough for all to hear, "Oh, I'm a 212."

Everyone froze around the table with forks in mid-air and mouths gaping open. The silence lasted. Finally, the hostess broke it by totally changing the subject and asking someone else something inane. The young Jewish man serenely continued to eat. The guy who told the 212 story simply looked at his plate and said nothing about it—ever again as far as I know.

The point? Words are powerful and never die. They begin to live when we say them. We have all devoutly wished, as I imagine my dining companion did, we could take our words back and swallow them quickly. We've all let words escape our unthinking and often unfeeling lips that we wished we could recall. The trick is to be sufficiently awake to avoid saying them in the first place.

Words take on a life of their own when they leave your lips.

Mistakes

— :: —

Often it takes some calamity to make us live in the present. Then suddenly we wake up and see all the mistakes we have made.

—Bill Watterson

It's really too bad, but that seems to be the way it is. We recognize our mistakes when something awful wakes us up and allows us to see things "the way they are."

My mistakes are only my mistakes when I see them as such, and not before. Until I recognize my errors, they are simply what I did, what I thought. In order to see my mistakes, something has to happen to wake me up, and that awakening invariably leads to one necessary thing: humility.

Now there's a virtue you don't hear much about these days. Humility is simply seeing things "the way they are." It comes from the Latin root *humus*, which means "earth," "soil." When you're humble, you see things plain as dirt, just the way they are.

Humility a virtue for our age—the age of spin-meisters, the age of marketing gurus, the age of double-speak politicians, the age of low levels of trust in those who lead, of those who speak to and for all of us. Get down to earth, please.

I recall a particular mistake of my past when I failed to say something I should have said. It was a mistake that hurt people. I thought I was doing the correct thing at the time. Then, after the "calamities" (someone lost a friend), I saw my error clearly. I ate dirt. Welcome to earth, to soil, to ground, to *humus*. It's really not a valid excuse to say, "I thought I was doing the right thing" (sweet refrain though it may be). The fact is that I was not doing the right thing. Why wait for calamities?!

No one can avoid mistakes. They are an essential ingredient in human life. But we must learn from them. The proper movement is from mistakes to humility. From blindness to earth. From doing wrong to recognizing the right. Wouldn't it be great if there were no calamities in the middle?

Do you need to eat dirt?

What Comes Next?

— :: —

It's like driving a car at night. You never see further than your headlights, but you can make the whole trip that way.

—E. L. Doctorow

Oh, how I needed to understand that lesson! At the time I needed it, I did not see it. The future looked empty, had no shape or form, and I was headed directly into it. I did not know what would come next.

But really, isn't all of life that way? We really never know what's coming next, what lies ahead—what challenges, what surprises, what disasters, what blessings. They are all out there somehow, ahead of us in the road, and our headlights don't reach very far.

Yet we manage to arrive nonetheless. We simply shine our lights onto whatever comes next on the road and approach it knowing we will somehow navigate the course. Then we refocus our lights ahead to reveal the next obstacle. All of life really is a bumbling through, even if we don't like to acknowledge it.

My own hardest bumbling came when I faced a major fork in the road. Both roads leading away were dark indeed. But even smaller trips can seem just as dark.

Does disaster await around the next corner? I don't feel that I have any control over that. My lights shine such a short distance ahead. The "what ifs" crowd my mind and exaggerate the dangers, obfuscate the advantages, and generally distract me from my purpose.

Yes, of course, we generally make it through. How? God only knows? All we can do is stay as awake as possible. I can only offer three thoughts on the journeys of our lives and they're not much of an offering:

1. Take your time before deciding; avoid compulsiveness;

2. Spend lots of quiet time alone;

3. Keep the end of your journey, why you're "going" there, clearly in your mind.

And, of course, remember Doctorow's insight: You only need to see a little ways ahead at any one moment.

Facing a fork in the road? Wake up.

Reality Show

— :: —

People often applaud an imitation and hiss the real thing.

—Aesop

I have watched several so-called reality shows on TV and can understand why many people find them entertaining. They are often fast-paced, seemingly unpredictable, and appear to feature folks just like you and me. It's reality.

Really? A reality show is defined as a "television program showing real people dealing with real situations." They range from programs depicting police operations and emergency rescues, to those in which people divorce, choose marriage partners, or actively deal with their personal problems on air.

I watched one reality show in which a young man went through the process of choosing a girlfriend from a field of several candidates. He chose the buxom blond and the two of them went off stage making eyes at each other and looking forward to their free stay at a plush Las Vegas resort. Did anyone really believe this was real?

Was anyone convinced that the final choice he made was the reality of his life and different from any other relationship he had? Did anyone really believe the relationship would last and be "special"?

I wouldn't mind so much if they called these shows something different—like "Let's Make Believe." The participants are all in the program for very real motives, but rarely, I believe, for the ones stated.

Please teach your children about this. Let them watch the shows; let them decide who gets voted off the island (are they still doing that?). But please explain to them that this is anything but real life. It's just like any other scripted and edited program. It just isn't quite as scripted. So hiss at reality shows, and then find some fine fictional drama to applaud. Where's Aesop when you need him?

> *This week, find something on TV to hiss, and something to applaud. And, if you can, help kids to see the difference.*

Taking a Shower

— :: —

The old folk crouching by their peat fires will tell their disbelieving grandchildren of standing naked mid-winter under jet streams of hot clean water.

— Ian McEwan

That will happen, McEwan suggests as an aside in his brilliant novel, *Saturday*, when this civilization has failed and the new Dark Ages have begun. I heartily agree that it will be an experience worth telling and remembering. Indeed, I believe it is an experience worth telling and remembering right now.

Taking a shower is one of those common occurrences that is, when you stop to consider it, an amazing one. To stand naked in a safe, warm, and private enclosure, with a cascade of hot clean water showering softly down upon you, bathing, refreshing, and cleansing. Amazing! McEwan's character continues to entrance the children gathered round the fire with tales of "lozenges of scented soaps and . . . viscous amber and vermillion liquids they rubbed into their hair to make it glossy and more voluminous than it really was, and . . . thick white towels as big as togas, waiting on warming racks."

In those future Dark Ages, the children listening around the peat fire will indeed be astonished, but so, I suggest, ought we.

The daily shower can become common, expected, unremarkable; like so many of our daily rituals, it can go by rushed, unnoticed, and under-appreciated.

Here is an invitation to awaken to the joys of showering with intention (the same for a bath, *mutatis mutandi*):

- ➤ Notice how the water feels as it physically flows on your body;

- ➤ Take a brief inventory on how you are feeling in general; remember what your day ahead holds for you, or perhaps recall memories of the day just ending;

- ➤ Feel appreciation for water—for safe water easily accessible in your home, for time to enjoy it, for cleanliness, and . . . .

Daily shower; daily joy.

The Old Ones

— :: —

The problem is never how to get the new, innovative thoughts into your mind, but how to get the old ones out.

—Dee Hock

Even though, at first glance, this may not look like much of an insight, I encourage you to take the advice to heart, especially if you face new kinds of problems. Hock knows the territory, having been instrumental in organizing and serving as CEO of a credit-card giant.

It's those old ideas. They are solidly lodged and at home in the way we think, in the patterns of our thought processes. They are comfortable in our heads, so they don't like to move.

They are so comfortable and at home that we are often unaware that they are there and in control. That possibility does not occur to us; they make sure of that. Oh, those old ones are clever!

It happened to me once, by default. I had a psycho-therapy client with whom I was making no progress; nothing seemed to move her in the direction we had established she needed to go. I was about to recommend that she see someone else when I thought to myself, *Nothing has worked so I may as well say to her what I've been thinking since the first time I met her. It won't help, but at least it won't hurt.*

From the beginning of our time together, I had a most unconventional and seemingly "crazy" kind of thought about this client that just popped into my head unbidden. It seemed, at the time, extraneous to any counseling process we were following. I told the client my thought, cautiously. And it was clearly the beginning of her change and growth.

"The old ones" finally gave way in my head, but not by any conscious decision on my part to get them out. It was simply a last-ditch, nothing-to-loose scenario. I have thought about that experience often as I continue to try to get the old ones out.

> *When facing a challenge, first "get the old ones out!"*

Stupid

— :: —

*Two things are infinite: the universe and human
stupidity; and I'm not sure about the universe.*

—Albert Einstein

The more I live, the more I realize that the line sepa-
rating stupidity and intelligence (borrowing a comparison from Solzhenitsyn) runs down the center of
every human mind. Yes, I am as often one of the "stupid" as I am one of the "intelligent." It all depends on
your point of view.

This morning, when the guy in front of me didn't
use his left-turn signal, he was a "stupid idiot." When I
do it, it's simply an oversight, a little forgetfulness, or my
passenger giving me directions too late. It, of course,
has nothing to do with my intelligence. However, for
the guy behind me, it has everything to do with my
stupidity.

What do you call the "stupid" people that come
in and out of your life? Consider it for a moment. Do
you see that, for others, you are frequently in that same
"stupid" category?

I'll not easily forget the time I considered a person "stupid" for taking a long and inconvenient route to a particular destination. "You went what way?" I asked her. "Why did you go that way? It's much easier and shorter to go this other way. You'd cut off a good half hour from your trip, save on gas, and besides the scenery is much better." That's what I said to her. What I thought was: "Stupid!"

"I went that way because there is a mud slide covering the highway on the other route and the road is impassible."

"Oh." How intelligent.

In other words, we too often define "stupidity" as anything that does not go along with our thinking, as anyone who does not see things from our point of view, as those who are not as informed as we are—whether or not we know all the facts!

Awaken to who is really "stupid"—and who isn't.

The Letter Opener

— :: —

My father and I both worked for your grandfather. He was a wonderful man; you can be very proud of him. Since you are his grandson, please take this letter opener . . .

—Hungarian-American upholsterer

The speaker above (I'm paraphrasing his words from memory) was a man in his sixties who had an upholstery business in the Buckeye Road area of Cleveland, Ohio. I was a twenty-year-old college student home on summer vacation. My mother asked me to take a chair to be re-upholstered. When the proprietor saw my family name, he asked if I was related to his former employer. "Yes," I said, "he was my grandfather." His appreciation and even devotion was immediately apparent. He insisted that I take the letter opener he had on his desk, which was from my grandfather's business and carried his logo. I received the brass opener gratefully and have kept it on my desk ever since.

Jump ahead fifty years—2007. In the meantime, I have inherited from my parents the same chair that I took to Buckeye Road. It looked the worse for its fifty years of wear. So I took it for the second time to be reupholstered, this time to a place near home in Berkeley, California. I was in the process of choosing material from a sample book. In the corner of my eye, I saw something I could not believe: my grandfather's letter opener sitting on the desk. How could that be, I thought? I didn't bring it with me, did I? I asked the upholsterer where he had gotten that letter opener.

"Oh, I found it in an old couch that I was working on and I didn't have one so I kept it for my desk to open my bills. Why?"

"That's from my grandfather!"

I had a hard time believing it. The same chair "produced" the same letter opener, in two upholstery shops, in two cities, 2000 miles and half a century apart! What are the chances of that? You wouldn't write it in a novel; it would stretch credibility too far.

When I told the whole story to the Berkeley upholsterer, he couldn't believe it either. Do you know what he said? He said, "Since you are his grandson, please take the letter opener!" Now I have two spontaneous, generous gifts that I can trace back to my grandfather!

Why do I tell you this story (I swear it's accurate!)? Because I believe there is a wake up call for me here, but I cannot figure out what it is.

(Can you help this guy out?)

Sexist Language

—— :: ——

Man's mind stretched to a new idea never goes back to its original dimensions.

—Gerald Holton

No, that's not a mistake. This is a repetition of an aphorism quoted earlier. But here, I want to make a different point that has to do with language. Holton talks about "man's" mind being stretched, not "woman's." He doesn't talk about "a person's" mind or "people's" minds, which could have carried the same collective meaning. He says "man's" mind. Period.

Holton uses sexist language here. Now, some may be annoyed at my pointing this out. Some may say it's not really sexist, that the masculine noun in English can mean both men and women. Yes, it can. But . . . .

It's simply one more expression of the dominant patriarchy, which is defined simply as control by males. It is also probable that those who think I am being too politically correct or annoyingly nit-picking do not consider the overarching patriarchy under which the world currently operates to be something that needs to be transformed.

To which I respectfully say, please wake up. Any perusal of the systems of the world shows that men are overwhelmingly in control. The opposite, of course, is matriarchy, which also must be avoided. Both extremes bring trouble—different kinds of trouble, but trouble nonetheless. The kinds of trouble we're in right now just happen to be the male kind.

Obviously, the unique powers of both men and women are essential, indeed beautiful. Balance is the goal. To achieve that, the weight of power in the world must continue to tip toward the feminine. Secure and observant men are not threatened; women continue to even the balance.

Name practical expressions of the patriarchy in your life? So?

Selfish

— :: —

For finally, we are as we love. It is love that measures our stature. There is no smaller package in the world than that of a person all wrapped up in himself.

—William Sloane Coffin

All of us can get "all wrapped up" in ourselves, can't we? It can happen in a split second, before we even know what's happened. There I am, all wrapped up in my issues and focused on how everything is going to affect me, me, me.

I think the only way to rout out selfishness—if that's even possible—is to incorporate its opposite into the very fabric of our lives.

There's an old movie that I have never been able to get out of my mind—*Magnificent Obsession* (1954). I must have been a teenager when I first saw it. It's not a great movie by any means, but its core theme struck me as remarkable: The secret to a happy life is to strive always to give to others abundantly and in secret. That's the magnificent obsession.

Jane Wyman and Rock Hudson act out that theme, sometimes in ways that would now be considered naïve and unbelievable. In the end, he "gets the girl" and disaster is avoided. But the theme remains compelling.

At the beginning of the film, Hudson's character is, to use Coffin's words, all wrapped up in himself. He causes great harm to others by his self-centered attitude. The heart of the film is his "conversion" and the story of how he works it out practically in his life. It's a study in selfishness recognized and transformed.

What I first remember feeling about the film is envy for the very single-mindedness and purposefulness of this character, and of the character (a "wise old man" archtype) from whom he learned it. I still admire generous and single-minded people.

What are some ways you incorporate the opposite of selfishness in your life? Take a moment to consider. There are many ways.

You may already have a magnificent obsession.

Working for Peace

—— :: ——

If you want to make peace, you don't talk to
your friends. You talk to your enemies.

—Moshe Dayan

Let's use the word "enemies" in the broad sense. The
work of peace is, I believe, first and foremost talking to
people with whom you disagree—mildly or violently. It
is available to literally all of us, all the time.

If you're politically blue, talk with someone who
is a convinced red-state dweller; if you're on the right,
seek out those on the left for a conversation; if you're
an agnostic, look for true religious believers and ask
some respectful questions; if you're a convinced dove,
go birding for an equally convinced hawk; if you are
devoutly religious, seek an atheist for conversation, not
for argument.

You get the idea. The things that divide us are
ubiquitous.

If you don't do this, you are not working for peace;
I don't care what your intellectual or spiritual convictions are. I have talked about this idea in several reflec-

tions and in several different ways because I believe it is so basic and so urgent.

Go out now, today, this afternoon or tomorrow morning to seek dialogue with someone who is very different from you. Take with you the attitudes of openness and attention and careful listening. See what you can learn; then see if you can teach something too. Leave behind the attitudes of "us/them;" bring along the attitude of "you and me/us."

Let's establish a U. S. Commission for Permanent Negotiations. Its purpose will be to perpetually encourage the process of bringing people of diverse convictions and practices to the point of mutual understanding and, if possible, respect.

This is something you can begin—or continue—right now, and never stop—never, because the work will never end. The only "excuse" is that you really don't want to work for peace, that peace is really not important to you.

The gauntlet is thrown!

Famous Last Words

— :: —

I'm just glad it'll be Clark Gable who's falling on his face and not Gary Cooper.

> —Gary Cooper, rejecting a role in *Gone with the Wind*

Louis Pasteur's theory of germs is ridiculous fiction.

> —Pierre Pachet, French professor of physiology

No flying machine will ever fly from New York to Paris.

> —Orville Wright, American inventor

If I had thought about it, I wouldn't have done the experiment. The literature was full of examples that said you can't do this.

> —Spencer Silver, inventor of Post-It Notes

Everything that can be invented has been invented.

> —Charles H. Duell, 19th-century U.S. patents commissioner

Who the hell wants to hear actors talk?

> —H.M. Warner, Warner Brothers Films

Stocks have reached what looks like a permanently high plateau.

—Irving Fisher, professor of economics

This "telephone" has too many shortcomings to be seriously considered as a means of communication. The device is inherently of no value to us.

—19th-century Western Union internal memo

The wireless music box has no imaginable commercial value. Who would pay for a message sent to nobody in particular?

—Response to David Sarnoff's proposal to invest in the radio

Drill for oil? You mean drill into the ground to try and find oil? You're crazy.

—Drillers enlisted by Edwin L. Drake, early oil man

We don't like their sound, and guitar music is on the way out.

—Decca Recording Co. rejecting The Beatles

Be sure you're awake before you speak.

References

— :: —

Birney, James. *The American Churches, The Bulwarks Of American Slavery*. New York: Masterson Press, 2008 (Originally 1885).

Carlson, Richard. *Don't Sweat the Small Stuff . . . and it's all small stuff*. New York: Hyperion, 1996.

Goleman, Daniel. *Emotional Intelligence: Why It Can Matter More Than IQ*. New York: Bantam, 2006.

Kundtz, David. *Nothing's Wrong: A Man's Guide to Managing His Feelings*. Boston: Conari Press, 2004.

———. *Quiet Mind: One-Minute Retreats from a Busy World*. Boston: Conari Press, 2004.

———. *Stopping: How to Be Still When You Have to Keep Going*. Berkeley, CA: Conari Press, 1998.

McEwan, Ian. *On Chesil Beach*. New York: Anchor, 2008.

———. *Saturday*. New York: Anchor, 2006.

O'Neill, Jamie. *At Swim, Two Boys: A Novel*. New York: Scribner, 2003.

Pasternak, Boris. *Doctor Zhivago*. New York: Signet, 1958.

Pollan, Michael. *In Defense of Food: An Eater's Manifesto.* New York: Penguin Press, 2008.

Prothero, Stephen. *Religious Literacy: What Every American Needs to Know—And Doesn't.* New York: HarperOne, 2008.

Rolvaag, Ole Edvart. *Giants in the Earth: A Saga of the Prairie.* New York: Harper Perennial Modern Classics, 1999 (Originally 1929).

Wilder, Thornton. *Our Town: A Play in Three Acts.* New York: Coward-McCann/Samuel French, Inc., 1938.

Permissions

—— :: ——

About the Author

David Kundtz has enjoyed several careers, including eighteen years in religious ministry and twenty years in the practice of psychotherapy, public speaking on stress and emotional health, and writing. He has graduate degrees in psychology and theology and a doctorate in pastoral psychology. He is the author of *Quiet Mind*, *Stopping*, *Moments in Between*, and several other books. He lives with his life partner in Kensington, CA and Vancouver, B.C. He can be reached through his Web site, *www.stopping.com*, or via e-mail, dk@stopping.com.

The author would like to acknowledge with thanks the kindness and competence of the Conari Press staff, especially Jan Johnson, Rachel Leach, and Jordan Overby.

To Our Readers

Conari Press, an imprint of Red Wheel/Weiser, publishes books on topics ranging from spirituality, personal growth, and relationships to women's issues, parenting, and social issues. Our mission is to publish quality books that will make a difference in people's lives—how we feel about ourselves and how we relate to one another. We value integrity, compassion, and receptivity, both in the books we publish and in the way we do business.

Our readers are our most important resource, and we value your input, suggestions, and ideas about what you would like to see published. Please feel free to contact us, to request our latest book catalog, or to be added to our mailing list.

Conari Press
An imprint of Red Wheel/Weiser, LLC
500 Third Street, Suite 230
San Francisco, CA 94107
www.redwheelweiser.com